SO YOU THINK YOU'RE A FILM BUFF?

Just about everyone knows that Humphrey Bogart DIDN'T say 'Play it again Sam' in *Casablanca*. But . . . did you know what *Casablanca* was called as a play? And who played the piano in *To Have and Have Not*?

These questions — and hundreds more — are posed (and answered) in SO YOU THINK YOU'RE A FILM BUFF? Tackle the questions for your own amusement . . . then produce the book at your next party and take the 'know all' look off the faces of your guests!

Max Hodes got hooked on the movies as a boy in Dunfermline, Fife. He's an award-winning columnist with the Daily Record *Scotland's largest-selling daily newspaper.*

SO YOU THINK YOU'RE A FILM BUFF?

More than
1,000 questions (and
answers) compiled by
Max Hodes

A STAR BOOK

published by
the Paperback Division of
W. H. ALLEN & Co. Ltd

A Star Book
Published in 1983
by the Paperback Division of
W. H. Allen & Co. Ltd
A Howard and Wyndham Company
44 Hill Street, London W1X 8LB

Reproduced, printed and bound in Great Britain by
Hazell Watson & Viney Ltd, Aylesbury, Bucks

ISBN 0 352 31352 8

For Jeannette
. . . and every other girl
in the back row who had
to watch the movie.

1. Catching up on 'Coop'

1. What was Gary Cooper's real name?

2. Name the film which won Cooper his first Oscar. *Sgt York*

3. In which film did Cooper star with Burt Lancaster? *Vera Cruz*

4. Who was Cooper's leading lady in *Love in the Afternoon*? *Audrey Hepburn*

5. In which film did Grace Kelly play the Quaker wife of Gary Cooper? *H. Noon*

6. Name the character Cooper played in *Mr Deeds Goes to Town.*

7. In which film did Marlene Dietrich appear with Cooper? *Desiry Rules Aget* X

8. Who directed the Gary Cooper film *Meet John Doe*? *John Ford.* X

9. In which film did Cooper play a baseball star?

10. What was Gary Cooper's last film?

2. Bushel and a Peck

1. Gregory Peck was nominated for an Oscar for only his second film. Title?

2. In which movie did Jane Wyman play Peck's wife? *The Yearling*

3. Who won an Oscar for Best Supporting Actress in the Gregory Peck film *Gentleman's Agreement*?

4. In which film did Peck play a British lawyer? *The Paradine Case or Affair*

5. For which film did Gregory Peck win an Oscar? *To Kill a Mocking Bird*

6. What Air Force rank did Peck hold in *Twelve O'Clock High*? *Wing Co*

7. In which Western did Peck play a gunslinger called Johnny Ringo? *The Gunfighter*

8. What part did Peck play in *Moby Dick*? *Capt Ahab.*

9. In which movie did Peck play a biblical king? *Solomon and Bathsheba*

10. For which Gregory Peck film did Audrey Hepburn win an Oscar? *Roman Holiday*

3. Remembering Grace Kelly

1. For which film did Grace Kelly win an Oscar? *Country Girl*

2. Grace Kelly met Prince Rainier on the Riviera while making which film? *To Catch a Thief*

3. Hitchcock starred Grace Kelly in three films. Titles? *Rear Window* *Dial M for Murder* *To Catch a Thief*

4. In which movie did Grace Kelly play opposite Alec Guinness?

5. Grace Kelly appeared in a remake of *Red Dust*. Film title?

6. For which picture did Grace Kelly receive a nomination for Best Supporting Actress?

7. Name the first film in which Grace Kelly appeared.

8. The Grace Kelly film *High Society* was a musical version of which play?

9. Who said Grace Kelly had 'sexual elegance'?

10. How old was Grace Kelly when she died? *50*

4. Take Ten

1. Alfred Hitchcock's first American movie won an Oscar for Best Picture. Title?

2. In which film did David Frost appear as himself?

3. Which cartoon character says 'What's up, Doc?'

4. Who starred in the 1980 remake of *The Jazz Singer*?

5. For which film, set in Mississippi, did Rod Steiger win an Oscar?

6. Who is Betty Perske better known as?

7. John Schlesinger won a Best Director Oscar for a film starring Dustin Hoffman and Jon Voight. Title?

8. Which U.S. President has been most often portrayed in films?

9. Marlon Brando refused to accept an Oscar for *The Godfather*. True or false?

10. Who played the rooftop violin solo in *Fiddler on the Roof*?

5. Beaming in on Bogart

1. What was Humphrey Bogart's middle name?

2. In which film did Bogart play a gangster called Nick 'Bugs' Fenner?

3. Who was the female star of the Bogart film *High Sierra*?

4. In which film did Bogart play a pseudo priest?

5. Name the private eye Bogart played in *The Maltese Falcon*.

6. For which three categories did *Casablanca* win Oscars?

7. *Casablanca* was originally a play. Title?

8. Who played the piano in the Bogart film *To Have and Have Not*?

9. In which film did Bogart play a washed-up movie director?

10. What was Bogart's last film?

6. Boning up on Bette

1. In which film did Bette Davis play a sluttish waitress?

2. Who directed Bette Davis in *The Letter*?

3. For which movie did Bette Davis win her first Oscar?

4. Which film propelled Bette Davis into stardom?

5. In which Bette Davis movie did Humphrey Bogart play a stable groom?

6. Who co-starred with Bette Davis in *Whatever Happened to Baby Jane?*

7. In which Bette Davis film did Claude Rains play a psychiatrist?

8. In which film did Bette Davis appear as herself?

9. Which Davis movie won seven Oscars?

10. In which Hammer film did Bette Davis star?

7. Latching on to Olivier

1. What was the original title of *The Prince and the Showgirl,* starring Laurence Olivier and Marilyn Monroe?

2. Name the character Olivier portrayed in *The Entertainer.*

3. Which Olivier film won Oscars for Best Actor and Best Picture?

4. In which film did Olivier play a supporting role as a police inspector?

5. Which general did Oliver portray in *Inchon*?

6. Who directed the Laurence Olivier — Michael Caine film *Sleuth*?

7. In which film did Olivier play an Arab tribal chieftain?

8. Which film established Olivier and Vivien Leigh as Britain's top romantic screen team?

9. In which Hollywood film was Olivier replaced by John Gilbert?

10. Who was Olivier's first wife?

8. Take Ten More

1. Glen Campbell appeared in a Western which won an Oscar for John Wayne. Title?

2. Cecil B. DeMille appeared as himself in which movie?

3. In which film did George Lazenby play James Bond?

4. Who is Nathan Birnbaum better known as?

5. Sir Compton Mackenzie appeared in the film of his book *Whisky Galore.* True or false?

6. The slogan 'Mean, Moody and Magnificent' was used to promote which movie?

7. For which film did Margaret Rutherford win an Oscar for Best Supporting Actress?

8. From which film is the last line: 'After all, tomorrow is another day . . .'?

9. Which character did Orson Welles portray in *The Third Man*?

10. In which movie did Audrey Hepburn play Holly Golightly?

9. A Finch of salt

1. In which film did Peter Finch appear with Gordon Jackson and Chips Rafferty?

2. Who did Finch play in *The Story of Robin Hood and his Merrie Men*?

3. In which film did Eileen Herlie play Finch's wife?

4. For which movie did Finch and Virginia McKenna win British Academy Film Awards for Best Actor and Best Actress?

5. Who directed Peter Finch in *Sunday Bloody Sunday?*

6. In which film did Finch play a Labour MP?

7. Which movie won Finch an Oscar?

8. In which film did Finch star with Sophia Loren?

9. What was Finch's last movie?

10. In which film did Finch play a Jewish antique dealer?

10. The answer's a Lemmon

1. Judy Holliday was in Jack Lemmon's first film. Title?

2. For which film did Lemmon win an Oscar for Best Supporting Actor?

3. Which actress was paired with Lemmon in *The Out-of-Towners*?

4. Who directed *Some Like It Hot?*

5. One Oscar was awarded to *Days of Wine and Roses*. Category?

6. Which Lemmon film became a TV series?

7. Lemmon directed a film starring Walter Matthau. Title?

8. Jack Lemmon won a 1973 Oscar for which film?

9. Who starred with Lemmon in *The April Fools*?

10. In which film did Lemmon wear a Mack Sennett moustache?

11. Clueing up on Cary Grant

1. What is Cary Grant's real name?

2. What was the stage title of the Cary Grant — Mae West film *She Done Him Wrong*?

3. Who was Grant's co-star in *Bringing Up Baby*?

4. On which well-known play was the Cary Grant film *His Girl Friday* based?

5. Name Cary Grant's first film for Hitchcock.

6. Who was Grant's female co-star in *Every Girl Should Be Married*?

7. Who directed the Cary Grant film *Operation Petticoat*?

8. In which film was Audrey Hepburn Cary Grant's co-star?

9. What was Grant's first film with Sophia Loren?

10. In which film did Cary Grant portray Cole Porter?

12. Who said it?

1. If I had as many love affairs as you fellows have given me credit for, I would now be speaking to you from inside a jar at the Harvard Medical School.

2. I deny I ever said actors are cattle. What I said was, 'Actors should be treated like cattle'.

3. I used to be Snow White, but I drifted.

4. Everything you see I owe to spaghetti.

5. Listen, I got three expressions: looking left, looking right, and looking straight ahead.

6. I'm not mean. I'm Scottish.

7. I once described my face as a cross between two pounds of halibut and an explosion in an old clothes closet.

8. I'm the only man who has a marriage licence made out To Whom It May Concern.

9. You think beautiful girls are going to stay in style forever?

10. It's kind of a sad thing when a normal love of country makes you a superpatriot.

13. Magic of Montgomery Clift

1. Which was the first movie in which Clift and Elizabeth Taylor appeared together?

2. What was Montgomery Clift's full name?

3. In which movie did Clift first play an American GI?

4. Clift played John Wayne's foster son in which film?

5. Olivia de Havilland won an Oscar in a film with Clift. Title?

6. *A Place in the Sun* was an adaptation of which novel?

7. Clift was in a film drama that won Oscars for Frank Sinatra and Donna Reed. Title?

8. During the making of which film did Clift have a near-fatal car crash?

9. Clift appeared in a film for which Maximilian Schell won an Oscar. Title?

10. What was Clift's last film?

14. Educating Rita

1. What was Rita Hayworth's real name?

2. Who did Rita marry during the making of *Cover Girl*?

3. In which espionage film did Rita co-star with Glenn Ford?

4. In which movie did Rita do the dance of the seven veils?

5. Which Rita Hayworth film was based on the story of London's Windmill Theatre?

6. Rita starred as the wife of a sadistic policeman in a trial drama. Title?

7. Jack Lemmon and Robert Mitchum were adventurers who fell for Rita in which movie?

8. Who wrote the songs for the Hayworth film *Pal Joey*?

9. Rita Hayworth starred in a film based on a Somerset Maugham story. Title?

10. In which musical did Adolphe Menjou play Rita's father?

15. Geeing up on Edward G.

1. What was Edward G. Robinson's real name?

2. Name the character Robinson played in the gangster film that made him a star, *Little Caesar*.

3. In which film did Robinson play a German doctor?

4. What was Robinson's hobby?

5. Robinson co-starred with Frank Sinatra in a movie. Title?

6. In which film did Robinson play the character Johnny Rocco?

7. Bette Davis co-starred with Robinson in a boxing movie. Title?

8. Which Robinson thriller did Orson Welles direct and play in?

9. Robinson made a movie on location in Kenya. Title?

10. Name Robinson's last film.

16. Tricky Ten

1. What was Diane Keaton's first film with Woody Allen?

2. What is Tony Curtis's real name?

3. *My Wicked Wicked Ways* was the title of an autobiography by which movie star?

4. For which movie did Robert Redford win an Oscar for Best Director?

5. In which film was Ursula Andress the leading lady of Elvis Presley?

6. By which name is Richard Jenkins better known?

7. Name the two rival gangs in *West Side Story*.

8. In which film does Barbra Streisand sing *People*?

9. Jack Nicholson plays a seedy radio personality in which movie?

10. Melvyn Douglas won an Oscar for Best Supporting Actor in a film starring Peter Sellers. Title?

17. Recalling Cagney

1. In which James Cagney film was Mae Clarke on the receiving end of a grapefruit?

2. Which role did Cagney play in *A Midsummer Night's Dream*?

3. What was Cagney's first Western?

4. In the Cagney film *The Strawberry Blonde,* who played the title role?

5. James Cagney's sister Jeanne appeared in *Yankee Doodle Dandy*. True or false?

6. Name two films in which Cagney appeared with Doris Day.

7. In which movie did Cagney co-star with Bette Davis?

8. Who was leading lady in *Angels With Dirty Faces*?

9. Apart from *Yankee Doodle Dandy,* in which other film did Cagney portray George M. Cohan?

10. In which movie did Cagney say 'You dirty rat!'?

18. Send for Sophia

1. Who made Sophia Loren into a star and married her?

2. Which film did Sophia make under Peter Ustinov's direction?

3. Sophia played a pizza vendor in her first film directed by Vittorio De Sica. Title?

4. In which film did Sophia co-star with Marlon Brando?

5. Which domestic comedy did Sophia make with Cary Grant?

6. From which novel was *The Pride and the Passion* adapted?

7. For which movie did Sophia win an Oscar?

8. Sophia played the daughter of Alec Guinness in which film?

9. Gregory Peck co-starred with Sophia in a thriller. Title?

10. Anthony Quinn was Sophia's leading man in three films. Titles?

19. Fonda memories

1. How many times was Henry Fonda married?

2. Name the character Fonda played in *The Grapes of Wrath*.

3. In which movie did Fonda play Wyatt Earp?

4. Fonda played Shirley Temple's father in a John Ford Western. Title?

5. Henry Fonda produced only one film. Title?

6. Fonda played the title role in *Mister Roberts*. True or false?

7. In which Alfred Hitchcock movie did Fonda star?

8. Name Fonda's epic Western with James Stewart.

9. In which World War II film did Fonda have a cameo role?

10. Fonda won an Oscar for his last movie. Title?

20. Trickier Ten

1. Who played Marilyn Monroe in *Goodbye Norma Jean*?

2. *The Fallen Idol* was from a book by Graham Greene. Title?

3. Who is Virginia McMath better known as?

4. Who wrote screenplays under the name Mahatma Kane Jeeves?

5. Mike Nichols won an Oscar for directing one of the most successful films of all time. Title?

6. Which actor portrayed, in different films, Sherlock Holmes and Dr Watson?

7. Who won an Oscar for Best Supporting Actress in *Paper Moon*?

8. Name the last 'Road' picture.

9. Who played the title role in *Scorpio*?

10. Who made his screen début in *Goodbye Columbus*?

21. Dial B for Barbara

1. In which Barbara Stanwyck film did Burt Lancaster play her murderous husband?

2. The Barbara Stanwyck film *Double Indemnity* was adapted from a short story by whom?

3. Barbara starred in the film of a Sean O'Casey play. Title?

4. Gary Cooper played a hobo in a film with Barbara. Title?

5. In which movie did Barbara co-star with Clifton Webb?

6. Barbara was nominated for an Oscar four times. Name the films.

7. In which Elvis Presley movie did Barbara appear?

8. Laurence Harvey and Jane Fonda appeared with Barbara in a 1962 film. Title?

9. Barbara appeared in a Western with Fred MacMurray. Title?

10. In which Preston Sturgess comedy did Barbara play a gold digger interested in wealthy Henry Fonda?

22. Harping on the Marx Brothers

1. Name the five original Marx Brothers.

2. What was Groucho's real name?

3. The Marx Brothers owed a lot to their legendary mother. Her name?

4. Who was one of the Marx Brothers' most famous film writers?

5. In which film does Groucho become President of Freedonia?

6. Who was leading lady in many Marx Brothers films?

7. In which Marx Brothers movie was the hilarious stateroom scene?

8. In which Marx Brothers film did Groucho sing *Hooray For Captain Spalding*?

9. Who was the real-life gambler of the Marx Brothers?

10. Which Marx Brothers movie climaxes with the breaking up of a moving train?

23. Checking up on Chaplin

1. Who was Charlie Chaplin's first wife?

2. In which part of London was Chaplin born?

3. One leading lady appeared in 35 Chaplin films. Name?

4. Which Chaplin movie is regarded as a classic?

5. What was Chaplin's first full-length film?

6. Chaplin established United Artists in 1919 with three others. Names?

7. Which Chaplin film was about a blind girl?

8. Name the two stars of the Chaplin-made film *A Countess From Hong Kong*.

9. Which 1928 film won Chaplin an Oscar?

10. How old was Chaplin when he died?

24. Even Trickier Ten

1. Kirk Douglas starred in a Walt Disney movie. Title?

2. Edythe Marrener won an Oscar for *I Want To Live*. Her screen name?

3. What have Roger Moore, George C. Scott and Peter Cook in common?

4. Which movie featured Anthony Quinn in an Oscar-winning role as the artist Gauguin?

5. James Cagney's last line was: 'Look, Ma — top of the world!' Which movie?

6. What have these films in common: *The Hasty Heart; King's Row; It's a Great Feeling*?

7. Who played President John F. Kennedy in *PT 109*?

8. Who said: 'I don't trust any bastard who doesn't drink.'?

9. Who played James Bond in *Diamonds are Forever*?

10. Which Beatle appeared in the David Essex film *That'll Be The Day*?

25. The Marvel of Marilyn

1. Who was Marilyn's first husband.

2. In which Marx Brothers film did Marilyn make a brief appearance?

3. Who was Marilyn's co-star in *The Seven-Year Itch*?

4. In which John Huston movie did Marilyn play a dumb blonde?

5. Marilyn did an exotic dance number, *Heat Wave,* in which film?

6. Joshua Logan directed Marilyn in probably her best movie. Title?

7. In which film did Marilyn play an unfaithful wife plotting to kill her husband?

8. Marilyn brought her playwright husband to Britain for the filming of *The Prince and the Showgirl*. His name?

9. Marilyn had a celebrated off-screen love affair with co-star Yves Montand during the making of which movie?

10. What was Marilyn's last film?

26. File on Flynn

1. What were Errol Flynn's middle names?

2. Olivia de Havilland co-starred with Flynn in many films. Name the first.

3. What was Flynn's first Western?

4. Errol Flynn never won an Oscar. True or false?

5. In which movie did Flynn do a song-and-dance number?

6. Flynn was Essex in *The Private Lives of Elizabeth and Essex*. Who played Elizabeth?

7. In which movie did Flynn play John Barrymore?

8. Orson Welles played a TV news personality in a Flynn film. Title?

9. In which film of an Ernest Hemingway novel did Flynn star?

10. Name the boxer Flynn portrayed in *Gentleman Jim*.

27. The Scarlett and Rhett Show

1. Who produced *Gone With The Wind*?

2. Name the character Leslie Howard played.

3. What was Vivien Leigh's real name?

4. Who played the part of Melanie?

5. Was *Gone With The Wind* made in black and white or Technicolor?

6. Who played Scarlett O'Hara's father?

7. Margaret Mitchell also wrote the screen version of *Gone With The Wind*. True or false?

8. Who played Scarlett's Mammy?

9. What role did Ward Bond play?

10. Clark Gable as Rhett Butler won one of the 10 Oscars which went to *Gone With The Wind*. True or false?

28. Heroic Heston

1. Charlton Heston played a circus manager in a film that won an Oscar for Best Picture. Title?

2. In which film spectacular did Heston co-star with Sophia Loren?

3. Heston won an Oscar for his role in a Roman epic. Title?

4. In which movie did Heston play Michelangelo?

5. Charlton portrayed General Gordon in which film spectacular?

6. Burl Ives won an Oscar for Best Supporting Actor in a Heston film directed by William Wyler. Title?

7. The Heston film *Planet of the Apes* was based on the book *Monkey Planet*. Author?

8. Heston named his son after the Scottish clan to which he belongs. Which is it?

9. Heston appeared in the same role in 'two pictures for the price of one.' Titles?

10. Geraldine Chaplin played Heston's wife in a film from a novel by James Michener. Title?

29. On Golden Hepburn

1. For which film did Katharine Hepburn win her first Oscar?

2. What was the last film in which Hepburn and Spencer Tracy appeared together?

3. In which movie did Hepburn co-star with Bob Hope?

4. Hepburn starred in a film based on a novel by Pearl Buck. Title?

5. Hepburn won an Oscar for *The African Queen*. True or false?

6. Judy Holliday appeared in a Hepburn-Tracy movie. Title?

7. In which film did Hepburn star as an athlete?

8. Burt Lancaster starred as a con man in a movie with Hepburn. Title?

9. In which film did Hepburn play a tourist in Venice who falls for Rossano Brazzi?

10. What was different about the Oscar that Hepburn won for *The Lion in Winter*?

30. The Lone Granger

1. What is Stewart Granger's real name?

2. Who was Granger's first wife?

3. In which film did Granger play a Sicilian gangster?

4. Granger had his first leading role in a film with Margaret Lockwood and James Mason. Title?

5. Granger played the violinist Paganini in *The Magic Bow*. Who really played the violin in the movie?

6. Who was Granger's leading lady in *King Solomon's Mines*?

7. In which film did Grace Kelly co-star with Granger?

8. Granger starred in a movie of a John Masters novel. Title?

9. Granger was a big hit in a swashbuckling film. Title?

10. Granger played opposite John Wayne in which adventure movie?

31. Tell me who

1. WHO played the title role in Ken Russell's *Valentino*?

2. WHO impersonated General Montgomery in *I Was Monty's Double*?

3. WHO played W.C. Fields in *W.C. Fields and Me*?

4. WHO played Buster Keaton in *The Buster Keaton Story*?

5. WHO won an Oscar for her portrayal of singer Loretta Lynn in *Coal Miner's Daughter*?

6. WHO played himself in *Abbott and Costello Meet the Keystone Kops*?

7. WHO said: 'I was a 14-year-old boy for 30 years.'?

8. WHO wrestled nude in *Women in Love*?

9. WHO said of whom: 'Wet she was a star.'?

10. WHO won Oscars for Best Actress in 1931 and Best Supporting Actress in 1970?

32. Mugging up on Mason

1. James Mason had his first screen success as the bad Lord Rohan in which film?

2. Who was Mason's first wife?

3. Mason was a hit as the tyrannical guardian of pianist Ann Todd in which movie?

4. Robert Newton played a drunken, crazy painter in which Mason film classic?

5. In which movie did Ava Gardner star with Mason?

6. Mason played Rommel in two movies. Titles?

7. Who starred with Mason in the espionage film *Five Fingers*?

8. Judy Garland sang *Born in a Trunk* in which Mason movie?

9. Mason appeared in a Disney film which won an Oscar for special effects. Title?

10. What was the name of the character Mason played in *Lolita*?

33. Just Gene

1. What is Gene Kelly's real name?

2. In which movie did Kelly dance with a mop?

3. Deanna Durbin appeared in a film with Kelly. Title?

4. Kelly danced with Jerry the cartoon mouse in which movie?

5. Kelly and Judy Garland were together in a 1948 musical, directed by Vincente Minelli. Title?

6. In which Kelly musical did Leslie Caron make her film début?

7. Natalie Wood starred with Kelly in a film from a novel by Herman Wouk. Title?

8. Which Barbra Streisand musical did Kelly direct?

9. Kelly played a newspaper reporter in a film drama with Spencer Tracy and Fredric March. Title?

10. Debbie Reynolds was Kelly's leading lady in which memorable musical?

34. A bash at Brando

1. Marlon Brando played a disabled war veteran in his first film. Title?

2. Vivien Leigh starred in a film with Brando and won an Oscar. Title?

3. In which movie did Brando play a Mexican folk hero?

4. Which role did Brando play in *Julius Caesar*?

5. Brando played the leather-jacketed leader of a motor-cycle gang in which film?

6. Which Elia Kazan movie won Brando an Oscar?

7. Brando played Napoleon in a 1954 film. Title?

8. In *Guys and Dolls*, Brando played Nathan Detroit. True or false?

9. In which movie was Brando both director and star?

10. Brando was Fletcher Christian in *Mutiny on the Bounty*. Who played Captain Bligh?

35. First things first

1. The first airline to introduce regular in-flight movies?

2. The first feature 'smellie'?

3. The first talkie made in Britain?

4. The first CinemaScope cartoon?

5. The first film in which Chaplin appeared as a tramp?

6. The first actress to win four Oscars?

7. The first hit song from a movie?

8. The first film to use Sensurround?

9. The first screen Tarzan?

10. The first co-stars to win Oscars for Best Actor and Best Actress?

36. One and only Woody

1. What is Woody Allen's real name?

2. Woody wrote the screenplay and appeared in a movie starring Peter Sellers. Title?

3. Which musical instrument does Woody play?

4. Which film did Woody direct, but not appear in?

5. Woody Allen appeared in *Casino Royale*. True or false?

6. Gene Wilder played a doctor in love with an Armenian sheep called Daisy in a Woody Allen film. Title?

7. Three Woody Allen books have been bestsellers. Titles?

8. As well as starring in *Play It Again, Sam,* Woody directed. True or false?

9. Which Woody Allen film has background music by Mendelssohn?

10. For which film did Woody win an Oscar for Best Director?

37. Forever Fontaine

1. Who is Joan Fontaine's actress sister?

2. For which Hitchcock movie did Fontaine win an Oscar for Best Actress?

3. Joan's first husband was a film actor. Name?

4. Who directed Fontaine in *Rebecca*?

5. Joan starred in *Jane Eyre*. Who played Rochester?

6. Who was Fontaine's leading man in *September Affair*?

7. Bing Crosby starred with Joan in a Billy Wilder film. Title?

8. Who was Fontaine's leading man in *A Certain Smile*?

9. In which country was Joan born?

10. Joan starred in a film shot in the West Indies, from a bestseller by Alec Waugh. Title?

38. Quite a Ladd

1. What was Alan Ladd's full name?

2. Sophia Loren made her first American film with Ladd. Title?

3. What relationship is Cheryl Ladd to Alan Ladd?

4. Who was Ladd's co-star in *This Gun For Hire*?

5. Raymond Chandler wrote the original screenplay of an Alan Ladd hit movie. Title?

6. In which film did Ladd have a walk-on part as a private eye for a gag?

7. In which classic Western did Ladd star?

8. What was the Alan Ladd film *The Red Beret* called in America?

9. How old was Ladd when he died?

10. What was his last film?

39. On the tip of your tongue

1. Three sailors were in the film *On the Town* — Frank Sinatra, Gene Kelly, and *who*?

2. Meryl Streep won an Oscar for Best Actress in *Kramer vs Kramer*. Truc or false?

3. What is Michael Caine's real name?

4. Who said: 'May the Force be with you?'

5. In which movie did Bob Hope appear as himself?

6. What was the first film in which Sean Connery played James Bond?

7. Who composed the music for *West Side Story*?

8. Who was the first actor to refuse to accept an Oscar?

9. With which film do you associate the song *The Windmills of Your Mind*?

10. Who is Mary Collins better known as?

40. Including Goldwyn out

1. What was Samuel Goldwyn's real name?

2. In which country was he born?

3. How many Oscars did his film, *The Best Years of Our Lives*, win?

4. What word is used to describe Goldwyn's mangling of the English language?

5. What well-known comedian owes his screen break to Goldwyn?

6. Who wrote the story on which *The Secret Life of Walter Mitty* was based?

7. *Wonderful Copenhagen* is one of the songs in *Hans Christian Andersen*. Who composed them?

8. Who played the Salvation Army girl in Goldwyn's *Guys and Dolls*?

9. In *Porgy and Bess*, who played Porgy?

10. How old was Goldwyn when he died?

41. Data on Deborah

1. In which country was Deborah Kerr born?

2. Her second husband is a writer. Name?

3. Deborah won an Oscar for *From Here to Eternity*. True or false?

4. In the film *Julius Caesar*, starring Marlon Brando, which role did Deborah play?

5. Name the movie in which Deborah was a widow engaged to David Niven.

6. Wendy Hiller won an Oscar for Best Supporting Actress in a movie starring Deborah Kerr. Title?

7. Deborah played Lady Fiona McTarry, otherwise Agent Mimi, in which film?

8. Peter Ustinov was Nero in a film epic with Deborah Kerr. Title?

9. Deborah starred in a film drama in which John and Hayley Mills appeared. Title?

10. Deborah starred as a nun with Robert Mitchum as a Marine in which movie?

42. Delving into DeMille

1. What was Cecil B. DeMille's first movie?

2. Who were his first partners?

3. What was his full name?

4. Charles Bickford played the lead in DeMille's first talkie. Title?

5. Gary Cooper's first film for DeMille was *The Plainsman*. What role did he play?

6. Who played the title roles in *Samson and Delilah*?

7. How many versions of *The Ten Commandments* did DeMille make?

8. Who played Moses in the 1956 version of *The Ten Commandments*?

9. How many Oscars did DeMille receive in his 45-year career?

10. What was his last film?

43. Ten Toughies

1. Christopher Lee played Sherlock Holmes's brother Mycroft in a film directed by William Wilder. Title?

2. Maggie Smith played a star who failed to win an Oscar . . . and won one as Best Supporting Actress. The film?

3. Who was Brigitte Bardot's first husband?

4. Who played Darth Vader in *Star Wars*?

5. Who is Walter Palannik better known as?

6. Who sang *Everybody's Talkin'* in *Midnight Cowboy*?

7. Who played the title role in *The Eyes of Laura Mars*?

8. Who starred as a motor tycoon in *The Betsy*?

9. Who was the first of the Fondas to win an Oscar?

10. Who said: 'Somebody put too many olives in my Martini last night.'?

44. Mindful of Mills

1. John Mills starred in a classic film, in which Alec Guinness made his screen début. Title?

2. Name the Mills children.

3. Mills starred in a Disney movie shot in Tobago. Title?

4. In which submarine movie did John Mills star?

5. John Mills won an Oscar for Best Supporting Actor in a film directed by David Lean. Title?

6. Under which name does Mrs John Mills write?

7. Hayley Mills made her screen bow in a movie starring her father. Title?

8. Name the title of the TV series in which John Mills plays a senior citizen?

9. Mills played a neurotic Army officer in a film based on a novel by James Kennaway. Title?

10. In which John Mills film did Richard Attenborough make his début as a director?

45. Best of Bronson

1. What is Charles Bronson's real name?

2. Bronson played a boxer in an Elvis Presley film. Title?

3. Bronson was one of *The Magnificent Seven*. True or false?

4. Lee Marvin starred in a hit World War II drama, in which Bronson played a convict. Title?

5. Bronson married his second wife in 1968. Her name?

6. What character did Bronson play in *The Valachi Papers*?

7. Bronson was a tunneller in a film set in a German prisoner-of-war camp. Title?

8. Which film made Bronson a star in America?

9. Bronson appeared in a supporting role in a horror movie starring Vincent Price. Title?

10. In which film starring Frank Sinatra and Dean Martin did Bronson appear?

46. Reaching for More

1. Kenneth More starred in a film about the sinking of the Titanic. Title?

2. What role did More play in *Scott of the Antarctic*?

3. In which comedy Western did Kenneth More star with Jayne Mansfield?

4. In which theatre did More start his career?

5. Kenneth More played the part of Ambrose Claverhouse in which classic comedy film?

6. Who wrote the biography of Douglas Bader, which became the movie *Reach For The Sky*?

7. In which film did More play opposite Susannah York?

8. Name the detective Kenneth More played in a TV series.

9. Which character did More play in the BBC television series *The Forsyte Saga*?

10. In *Genevieve*, who really played the trumpet for Kay Kendall?

47. Who, which, what?

1. Who played Agatha Christie's detective, Miss Marple, in *The Mirror Crack'd*?

2. Which boxing film won Robert De Niro an Academy Award for Best Actor?

3. Which female star from TV's *Dallas* appeared in *The Life and Times of Judge Roy Bean*?

4. Who played Eric Liddell in *Chariots of Fire*?

5. *The Postman Always Rings Twice* was from a story by whom?

6. Whose clothes for *My Fair Lady* won an Oscar?

7. Jane Fonda and Dolly Parton were two of the office girls in *Nine to Five*. Who was the third?

8. Who directed *The Shining*?

9. Lloyd Bridges and Robert Stack appeared in a 1980 air 'disaster' spoof movie. Title?

10. Who played Clint Eastwood's girl friend in *Bronco Harry*?

48. Magnificent Marvin

1. For which off-beat Western did Lee Marvin win an Oscar for Best Actor?

2. Which character did Marvin play in *The Dirty Dozen*?

3. Marvin starred with Paul Newman in a downbeat Western. Title?

4. Who said of Marvin: 'I'm not his psychiatrist. I don't know whether he has one or needs one. I'm only saying that, to understand him, one needs help.'?

5. Marvin appeared in a film for which Montgomery Clift received an Academy Award Nomination. Title?

6. In which movie did Sissy Spacek appear with Marvin?

7. Marvin starred with Burt Lancaster and Claudia Cardinale in a ripsnorting adventure film. Title?

8. Which movie gave Marvin a No. 1 single for *Wanderin' Star*?

9. Lee Marvin played Liberty Valance in *The Man Who Shot Liberty Valance*. True or false?

10. Marvin and Roger Moore co-starred in an adventure movie based on a novel by Wilbur Smith. Title?

49. Brush up your Barbra

1. Which Barbra Streisand movie won an Oscar for Best Song?

2. Yves Montand co-starred with Streisand in a film directed by Vincente Minnelli. Title?

3. In which movie did Barbra sing *Don't Rain On My Parade*?

4. Peter Bogdanovich directed Streisand in a comedy with Ryan O'Neal. Title?

5. In which film did Barbra team up with George Segal?

6. Streisand starred in one of the first American movies to deal with women's rights. Title?

7. Barbra formed a film company called First Artists. Who were her first two partners?

8. Who produced the Streisand film *A Star Is Born*?

9. Barbra's film *Yentl* is based on a short story by a Nobel Prize-winning author. Name?

10. Did Streisand and her first husband, Elliott Gould, have any children?

50. A note to Bing

1. What was Bing Crosby's real name?

2. Name the group in which Bing first sang.

3. For which movie did Crosby win an Academy Award for Best Actor?

4. Who was Bing's first wife?

5. How many 'Road' films did Crosby make with Bob Hope?

6. Bing appeared in *The Princess and the Pirate*. True or false?

7. In which movie did Crosby first sing *White Christmas*?

8. Name Bing's first film in Technicolor.

9. In which movie did Crosby sing *The Waiter, The Porter and the Upstairs Maid*?

10. Bing starred in a film adaptation of a Mark Twain novel. Title?

51. Ten to test you

1. In which film did the Oscar-winning song *The Shadow of Your Smile* feature?

2. John Wayne and Katharine Hepburn co-starred in a 1975 Western. Title?

3. What is Peter O'Toole's full name?

4. Who is Shirley Beaty better known as?

5. Charles Bronson starred in the film of an Alistair MacLean novel. Title?

6. Who said: 'Bring on the empty horses'?

7. Who was the first Italian to win an Oscar?

8. Who sang *Raindrops Keep Fallin' On My Head* in *Butch Cassidy and the Sundance Kid*?

9. How old was Shirley Temple when she appeared in her first film?

10. The film *The Railway Children* was an adaptation of a story by E. Nesbit. Its title?

52. Looking to your Laurel and Hardy

1. What was Stan Laurel's real name?

2. Name Laurel and Hardy's first feature film.

3. What was Oliver's favourite line to Stanley?

4. Who launched Stan Laurel's screen career?

5. What was Ollie's offscreen nickname?

6. In which movie did Laurel and Hardy join the Foreign Legion?

7. Name Laurel and Hardy's most successful film.

8. In which movie did Stan and Ollie sing *In the Blue Ridge Mountains of Virginia, On the Trail of the Lonesome Pine*?

9. What was Laurel and Hardy's last American film?

10. For what did Stan win a special Academy Award?

53. Swotting up on Sinatra

1. In which movie did Frank Sinatra sing *I Couldn't Sleep a Wink Last Night*?

2. Name the character Sinatra played in his Oscar-winning performance in *From Here To Eternity*.

3. Sinatra and Gene Kelly starred as sailors on leave in a 1945 musical. Title?

4. Sinatra was one of the stars of *Guys and Dolls,* which was based on a story by whom?

5. Louis Armstrong played himself in which Sinatra film?

6. Sinatra was in *Around the World in Eighty Days.* True or false?

7. Frankie Laine and Lena Horne made guest appearances in which Sinatra movie?

8. Who played Sinatra's parents in *Come Blow Your Horn*?

9. Which film did Sinatra star in and direct?

10. Name the first joint movie appearance of Sinatra and the Clan.

54. Fangs for the Christopher Lee memory

1. Christopher Lee played the painter Seurat in which movie?

2. Errol Flynn and Christopher Lee fought a duel in which film?

3. Lee appeared in *Scott of the Antarctic.* True or false?

4. In which film adaptation of *Dr Jekyll and Mr Hyde* did Christopher Lee star?

5. Name the Hammer film in which Lee and Peter Cushing first appeared together?

6. In which movie about Rasputin did Christopher Lee star?

7. Lee appeared as the hit man Scaramanga in which James Bond film?

8. What was the first movie in which Lee played Dr Fu Manchu?

9. Evelyn Laye appeared in a whodunit starring Christopher Lee. Title?

10. In which Hammer film, based on a story by Arthur Conan Doyle, did Lee star with Peter Cushing?

55. Ten more to test you

1. Who is Mia Farrow's actress mother?

2. Shirley MacLaine's first starring role was in a film opposite Frank Sinatra. Title?

3. Name Charles Chaplin's first film in colour.

4. What was the first movie Paul Newman made with Joanne Woodward?

5. Who was nicknamed *The Man You Love to Hate*?

6. *Storm Over the Nile* was a remake of which original?

7. Who received an Oscar for Best Actor for *The Goodbye Girl*?

8. Who played the Jackal in *The Day of the Jackal*?

9. What do the initials D. W. stand for in D. W. Griffith?

10. Jason Robards won an Oscar two years running for Best Supporting Actor. Name the films.

56. Close-up on Clint

1. Which Spaghetti Western made Clint Eastwood an international star?

2. Name the character Eastwood played in TV's *Rawhide*.

3. Lee Marvin co-starred with Eastwood in a hit musical. Title?

4. Clint and Richard Burton posed as Nazi officers in which World War II drama?

5. In which movie did Eastwood star as a disc jockey and make his bow as a director?

6. Clint played the title role in *Dirty Harry*. What was Harry's surname?

7. Eastwood directed a film starring William Holden, but stayed offscreen. Title?

8. Which Clint Eastwood film climaxed in the Swiss Alps?

9. Name the movie in which Clint had an orang-utan as mate.

10. As well as starring in *High Plains Drifter,* Eastwood also directed. True or false?

57. Hope springs eternal

1. What is Bob Hope's real name?

2. What was Hope's first 'Road' picture?

3. In which movie did Hope say: 'I'll take a lemonade — in a dirty glass.'?

4. Which Hope film featured the Oscar-winning song *Buttons and Bows*?

5. The Hope film *Sorrowful Jones* was based on a Shirley Temple movie. Title?

6. Marilyn Maxwell was Hope's leading lady in a film from a story by Damon Runyon. Title?

7. Hope played Eddie Foy in *The Seven Little Foys*. Who played Mrs Foy?

8. Hope played a Broadway critic in a film with Lucille Ball. Title?

9. Phyllis Diller was a wacky maid in which Hope movie?

10. How many special Oscars have been awarded to Bob Hope?

58. Memory teasers

1. In which film did Buster Keaton and Charles Chaplin work together for the first and last time?

2. Whose story was featured in *Somebody Up There Likes Me*?

3. In which 'Road' film did the Andrews Sisters appear as themselves?

4. In the 1966 remake of *Stagecoach,* who took the Thomas Mitchell role of the alcoholic doctor?

5. Who played showman Billy Rose in *Funny Lady*?

6. In *The Happy Hooker,* who played the title role?

7. In which movie did John Wayne play a Chicago cop operating in Britain?

8. Who was Lee Jacob better known as?

9. Which famous missionary's story was told in *The Inn of the Sixth Happiness*?

10. In which movie did Peter Ustinov and his daughter Pavla appear together as father and daughter?

59. Bogarde on the spot

1. What is Dirk Bogarde's real name?

2. Name Bogarde's first film with director Joseph Losey.

3. Bogarde and Julie Christie won British Academy Awards for which movie?

4. In which picture did Dirk play a lawyer?

5. Judy Garland made her last film with Bogarde. Title?

6. In which Hollywood movie did Dirk play Franz Liszt?

7. Bogarde portrayed Simon Sparrow in four 'Doctor' films. Titles?

8. Name the character Dirk played in *Death in Venice*.

9. In which movie did Charlotte Rampling co-star with Bogarde?

10. Dirk starred in a World War I film about a trial for desertion. Title?

60. Russell of spring

1. Ken Russell directed the film of a Len Deighton book. Title?

2. Glenda Jackson won her first Oscar for Best Actress in a movie directed by Ken Russell. Title?

3. In the Ken Russell film *The Music Lovers,* who played composer Peter Tchaikovsky?

4. Vanessa Redgrave starred in Russell's movie, *The Devils.* What role did she play?

5. In which Ken Russell musical did Glenda Jackson make a guest appearance?

6. Dorothy Tutin sang her own song, *Two Fleas,* in which Ken Russell film?

7. In *Mahler,* directed by Russell, who played Gustav Mahler?

8. Which Beatle played the Pope in Ken Russell's *Lisztomania*?

9. Who was the Pinball Wizard in the Ken Russell movie *Tommy*?

10. Jack Nicholson was in *Tommy.* True or false?

61. Quiz on Quinn

1. Where was Anthony Quinn born?

2. What was Quinn's first film?

3. For which two films did Quinn win Oscars for Best Supporting Actor?

4. In which Gary Cooper Western did Quinn appear?

5. Who was Quinn's first wife?

6. Lila Kedrova won an Oscar for Best Supporting Actress in a celebrated Anthony Quinn movie. Title?

7. Which Anthony Quinn picture, set in Italy, won an Oscar for Best Foreign Film?

8. Quinn appeared in a World War II adventure film, shot on location in the Greek Isles. Title?

9. Mickey Rooney was in a boxing film which starred Anthony Quinn. Title?

10. David Lean won a Best Director Academy Award for a film spectacular in which Quinn appeared. Title?

62. More memory teasers

1. Which film was chosen for the first Royal Film Performance in 1946?

2. In which Western did Inger Stevens co-star with Clint Eastwood?

3. The cast of a well-known circus was used in *The Greatest Show on Earth.* Which circus?

4. What was George Segal's first movie with Glenda Jackson?

5. Bob Hope played Jimmy Walker, Mayor of New York, in which movie?

6. Charles Chaplin won an Oscar for the music score of one of his films. Title?

7. What was the classical background music to *Brief Encounter*?

8. Who starred in the Western *Bite the Bullet*?

9. Mel Brooks starred in and directed a spoof movie about Hitchcock. Title?

10. Who played the gang leader in *Dog Day Afternoon*?

63. Paging Poitier

1. Sidney Poitier played a young priest in a movie set in Africa. Title?

2. In which film did Poitier play a juvenile delinquent?

3. Poitier played Clark Gable's son in a movie. True or false?

4. Poitier and Tony Curtis were prisoners on the run in a Stanley Kramer film. Title?

5. Did Poitier really sing in *Porgy and Bess*?

6. For which picture did Poitier win an Oscar for Best Actor?

7. Anne Bancroft starred with Poitier in a film about a crisis clinic. Title?

8. Lulu appeared with Poitier in a movie and had a hit record of the title. Name it.

9. In which film with Rod Steiger did Poitier play a detective?

10. Name the play which gave Poitier his greatest success on Broadway.

64. Taylor-made

1. Elizabeth Taylor achieved screen stardom at the age of 12. The film?

2. Who was Elizabeth's first husband?

3. In which movie did Elizabeth play Michael Caine's wife?

4. Elizabeth and Marlon Brando starred in a film from a novel by Carson McCullers. Title?

5. Elizabeth won two Oscars for Best Actress. Name the films.

6. James Dean appeared in his last film with Elizabeth. Title?

7. Burl Ives won an Oscar for his performance in the Elizabeth Taylor film *Cat on a Hot Tin Roof*. True or false?

8. Elizabeth and Richard Burton starred in a film adapted from a novel by Graham Greene. Title?

9. Elizabeth Taylor was in *Quo Vadis?* True or false?

10. Director George Stevens won Oscars for two films in which Elizabeth Taylor starred. Titles?

65. Raising Caine

1. Michael Caine came to notice for his performance in which epic film?

2. As a result of which movie was Caine dubbed Mr Sex-in-Specs?

3. Caine has twice been nominated for an Oscar. Name the films.

4. In which movie did Caine play a homicidal maniac?

5. Caine played agent Harry Palmer in three films from Len Deighton books. Titles?

6. In which movie did Caine play a thriller writer?

7. Caine co-starred with Sidney Poitier in an adventure film set in South Africa. Title?

8. Who played Caine's rogue compatriot in *The Man Who Would Be King*?

9. Name the world-famous footballer who appeared with Caine in *Escape to Victory*.

10. Caine played a German in two films. One was *The Eagle Has Landed*. What was the other?

66. Still more memory teasers

1. The Oscar-winning song *In the Cool, Cool, Cool of the Evening* was sung by Bing Crosby in which picture?

2. In *The Gold Rush,* Charlie Chaplin ate his boot. What was it really made of?

3. Who won an Oscar for Best Supporting Actress in *Bonnie and Clyde*?

4. Who played a Nazi war criminal in *The Boys From Brazil*?

5. A 1924 costume film, which starred Rudolph Valentino, was remade starring Bob Hope. Title?

6. Which film do you associate with the Oscar-winning song *All the Way*?

7. Who is Issur Danielovitch Demsky better known as?

8. Who played the police chief in *Jaws* and *Jaws 2*?

9. Name the detective played by Gene Hackman in *The French Connection* and *French Connection 2*.

10. Which Laurel and Hardy film won an Academy Award?

67. Label it Huston

1. What is John Huston's middle name?

2. Name the first film Huston directed.

3. For which movie did John Huston and his father, Walter Huston, win Oscars for Best Director and Best Supporting Actor?

4. Marilyn Monroe appeared in a 1950 film directed by John Huston. Title?

5. Who won an Oscar for the John Huston film *The African Queen*?

6. Who played Toulouse-Lautrec in the Huston movie *Moulin Rouge*?

7. Claire Trevor won an Oscar for Best Supporting Actress in a film directed by Huston. Title?

8. James Robertson Justice was in Huston's *Moby Dick*. True or false?

9. Huston directed Stacy Keach as a washed-up boxer in which movie?

10. Who wrote the screenplay of the John Huston film *The Misfits*?

68. Just Jane

1. What is Jane Fonda's middle name?

2. Jane won an Oscar for *Klute*. Who was her co-star?

3. Name the film about marathon dance contests in which Jane starred.

4. Who is Jane's second husband?

5. Name the Jane Fonda film which was inspired by the Kinsey Report.

6. Who was Jane's partner in crime in *Fun with Dick and Jane*?

7. Jack Lemmon won an Oscar for a film in which Jane played a TV newscaster. Title?

8. In which film did Jane co-star with Alan Alda?

9. Name the movie which won Oscars for Jane Fonda and Jon Voight.

10. Vanessa Redgrave won an Oscar for Best Supporting Actress in a film which starred Jane Fonda. Title?

69. Mad Mel

1. What is Mel Brooks's real name?

2. Brooks made his name writing for which American comedian?

3. Name Mel's first feature film.

4. In which film did Mel Brooks have a cameo role as a German scientist?

5. Brooks won Oscars for which two films?

6. Which Mel Brooks movie is set in Russia in the 1920s?

7. Gene Wilder played the Waco Kid in one of his most celebrated films. Title?

8. Marty Feldman played the hunchback Igor in a movie which Mel Brooks directed and starred in. Title?

9. Liza Minnelli appeared as herself in a Mel Brooks film. Title?

10. In which Mel Brooks movie did Pamela Stephenson appear?

70. Try these for size

1. For which film did director Billy Wilder win his first Oscar?

2. James Dean died at 24. What caused his death?

3. Who composed the music for the Harrison Ford movie *Blade Runner*?

4. Who wrote the novel on which *The Blue Lagoon* was based?

5. In which movie did Robert Redford play a prison governor?

6. Which American TV actress directed *Can't Stop The Music*?

7. Peter Ustinov is the second screen Charlie Chan. Who played the first?

8. Where was the science fiction movie *Death Watch* shot?

9. Which film do you associate with the Oscar-winning song *Chim Chim Cheree*?

10. Which composer was the subject of the movie *Till the Clouds Roll By*?

71. Beaming in on Burt

1. What is Burt Reynolds's full name?

2. Which movie put Reynolds on the road to stardom?

3. Rachel Ward was in a film which Reynolds starred in and directed. Title?

4. Roger Moore, Dean Martin and Sammy Davis Jr. appeared in a hit 1981 movie starring Reynolds. Title?

5. How many *Smoky and the Bandit* films did Reynolds star in?

6. Reynolds played himself in a movie directed by Mel Brooks. Title?

7. Has Reynolds ever won an Oscar?

8. Reynolds starred as a train robber in a Western co-starring Sarah Miles. Title?

9. Reynolds appeared in *Everything You Always Wanted to Know About Sex*. True or false?

10. Which movie about stuntmen did Reynolds star in?

72. Be sure of Shelley

1. What is Shelley Winters's real name?

2. Shelley sang with Frank Sinatra in which movie?

3. In which Western did Shelley appear with James Stewart?

4. Who was Shelley's first husband?

5. Shelley said of whom: 'He was the finest actor I ever worked with — and somehow the loneliest.'?

6. Charles Laughton directed only one film, in which Shelley appeared. Title?

7. Shelley won two Oscars for Best Supporting Actress. Name the films.

8. Robert De Niro appeared as one of Shelley's four sons in which movie?

9. In which British film did Shelley star with Ralph Richardson?

10. In *The Poseidon Adventure,* Shelley played a middle-aged Jewish woman. Who played her husband?

73. Know your Niven

1. Name an early David Niven comedy with Ginger Rogers.

2. An Otto Preminger film put Niven on the road to success. Title?

3. For which movie did Niven win his one and only Oscar?

4. In which 'Road' film did Niven appear briefly as a Tibetan monk?

5. What was the title of Niven's first chapters of autobiography?

6. Niven played a test pilot in *The First of the Few*. What was the film called in America?

7. Which historical film was a millstone, rather than a milestone, in Niven's career?

8. In which movie did Niven appear with Mario Lanza?

9. Niven and June Allyson starred in a remake of a Thirties comedy which featured William Powell and Carole Lombard. Title?

10. Which role did Niven play in *Around the World in Eighty Days*?

74. Who said this?

1. When you're born a cockney, there's no way to go but up.

2. In Europe, an actor is an artist. In Hollywood, if he isn't working, he's a bum.

3. I was terribly gauche and so tense I don't know how people could stay in the room with me.

4. Not since Attila the Hun swept across Europe, leaving 500 years of total blackness, has there been a man like Lee Marvin.

5. The minute you feel you have given a faultless performance is the time to get out.

6. I haven't aged into a character actor. I'm still an old leading man.

7. The monster was the best friend I ever had.

8. People think all I have to do is to stand up and tell a few jokes. But every year it gets a bit more difficult to stand up.

9. The audience knows the truth, not the critics. That's why those are the people I care about pleasing.

10. My own personality is so vapid and bland, I have to go steal the personalities of other people to be effective on the screen.

Marley's ghost in *Scrooge*. His name?
WENTIETH CENTURY-FOX

2. (above) Two famous faces from the past in *Airport 1975*. Their names?   CIC

3. (Below) Simon Ward was a vet in *All Creatures Great and Small*. Who played his wife?   EMI

4. (Above) Dustin Hoffman and Robert Redford in *All the President's Men*. Who played their editor (centre)? COLUMBIA/WARNER

5. (Below) Edward Fox tries out a rifle in *The Day of the Jackal*. The actor behind played the gunsmith. His name? CIC

6. The film is *The Eagle Has Landed*. Who played Admiral Canaris (left) and

75. Astaire is born

1. Who was Fred Astaire's first dance partner?

2. In a Fred Astaire film, *The Continental* was the first number to win an Oscar for Best Song. Name the movie.

3. Jack Buchanan featured in a Fred Astaire musical. Title?

4. In which film did Astaire do a gravity-defying dance all over the ceilings and walls?

5. Leslie Caron played a French war orphan in which Astaire musical?

6. Name the movie in which Petula Clark played Astaire's daughter.

7. For what did Astaire win a special Oscar in 1950?

8. A pair of white shoes danced by themselves in which Astaire film?

9. Name the film in which Astaire played his first dramatic role.

10. In which 'Disaster' movie did Astaire play a confidence trickster?

76. Recalling Bacall

1. Lauren Bacall was given a screen test after appearing on the cover of which magazine?

2. Name the first movie in which Bacall appeared with Humphrey Bogart.

3. In which film did Bacall play Lionel Barrymore's daughter?

4. Humphrey Bogart was Bacall's first husband. Who was her second?

5. Humphrey Bogart played a tough private eye in a movie with Bacall. Title?

6. Bacall was one of three gold diggers in *How to Marry a Millionaire*. Who played the other two?

7. Dorothy Malone won an Oscar for Best Supporting Actress in a film starring Bacall and Rock Hudson. Title?

8. Bacall played a fashion designer in a movie with Gregory Peck. Title?

9. Bacall and Paul Newman starred in a version of Ross Macdonald's book *The Moving Target*. Title?

10. Ingrid Bergman won an Oscar for Best Supporting Actress in a movie in which Bacall appeared. Title?

77. Preminger presents

1. Otto Preminger directed Gene Tierney in a 1944 movie, which led to his landing a long-term Hollywood contract. Name the film.

2. Preminger played a German prison commandant in a film directed by Billy Wilder. Title?

3. Which Preminger movie was banned by the Catholic church?

4. Marilyn Monroe played a saloon singer caught up in the gold rush in which Preminger film?

5. Diahann Carroll appeared in two Preminger films. Titles?

6. Who played opposite Frank Sinatra in Preminger's *The Man With the Golden Arm*?

7. Leon Uris, author of *Exodus,* also scripted the Preminger film. True or false?

8. *Advise and Consent,* directed by Preminger, was based on a novel by whom?

9. Otto's fellow director, John Huston, had his first major role in a Preminger film. Title?

10. In which Preminger movie did Laurence Olivier play a supporting role?

78. Search your memory (1)

1. Who played the title role in *The Elephant Man*?

2. In which movie did Peter Sellers make his final appearance?

3. Topol appeared in a James Bond film. Title?

4. Who played the title role in *Popeye*?

5. In *Raging Bull,* Robert De Niro gave an Oscar-winning performance as which boxer?

6. Name the movie by Roman Polanski which won Oscars for art direction, costume and cinematography?

7. In which Jack Lemmon film did Barry Manilow sing *We Still Have Time*?

8. Dudley Moore wrote The Ten Commandments in which comedy movie?

9. Who was Laszlo Loewenstein better known as?

10. Olivia Newton-John appeared in her second movie with Gene Kelly. Title?

79. My Guinness!

1. In which film did Alec Guinness play Disraeli?

2. Guinness played Fagin in *Oliver Twist*. Who was the Artful Dodger?

3. In which movie did Guinness portray eight different characters?

4. What do Guinness and Frank Sinatra have in common?

5. For which film did Guinness win an Oscar for Best Actor?

6. J. B. Priestley wrote the screenplay of a comedy-drama starring Guinness. Title?

7. Name two films in which Guinness played an Army officer.

8. An Alec Guinness comedy won an Oscar for writer T. E. B. Clarke. Title?

9. Guinness starred with Grace Kelly in her last film before retiring. Title?

10. Name the character Guinness played in *Star Wars* and *The Empire Strikes Back*.

80. Garland for July

1. What was Judy Garland's real name?

2. Name Judy's first full-length film.

3. Which singing star played Judy's mother in *Broadway Melody of 1938*?

4. Name Judy's first film with Mickey Rooney.

5. Who was Judy's first husband?

6. For which movie did Judy win a special Oscar?

7. Name the first Judy Garland film directed by Vincente Minnelli.

8. Who replaced Judy in *Annie Get Your Gun*?

9. Judy was a guest star in a wartime musical starring Kathryn Grayson. Title?

10. In which movie did Judy and Gene Kelly sing *Be a Clown*?

81. Know your Newman

1. Paul Newman's first movie was a flop. Title?

2. In *Somebody Up There Likes Me,* Newman played boxer Rocky Graziano. Who played his wife?

3. George Kennedy won an Oscar for Best Supporting Actor in a Paul Newman film. Title?

4. In which movie did Newman play a pool shark called Fast Eddie?

5. Both Paul Newman and his wife Joanne Woodward have won Oscars. True or false?

6. Burl Ives played Big Daddy in a Paul Newman film. Title?

7. What is Newman's favourite sport?

8. Patricia Neal and Melvyn Douglas won Oscars for their performances in a Paul Newman film. Title?

9. Newman's first movie as a director starred Joanne Woodward. Title?

10. Scott Joplin's music was the background to one of Newman's greatest successes. Title?

82. Search your memory (2)

1. Mae West and George Raft appeared on the screen for the last time in which movie?

2. Who played 'M' in the James Bond movies?

3. Mary Steenburgen won a 1980 Oscar for Best Supporting Actress in which film?

4. In which picture about motor-cycle racing did David Essex star?

5. She played Olive Oyl in *Popeye,* and starred with Jack Nicholson in *The Shining*. Name?

6. Goldie Hawn, as well as starring in *Private Benjamin,* also produced it. True or false?

7. Who played the ruthless film director in *The Stunt Man*?

8. Who starred as a farm boy in the big city in *Urban Cowboy*?

9. In which movie was the Oscar-winning song *Call Me Irresponsible* featured?

10. Which character have both Elvis Presley and Edward G. Robinson portrayed on the screen?

83. The Duke

1. What was John Wayne's real name?

2. Thomas Mitchell won an Oscar for Best Supporting Actor in a John Wayne film. Title?

3. Name the movie which Wayne produced, directed and starred in.

4. For which film did Wayne win an Oscar for Best Actor?

5. In which country was the John Wayne film *The Quiet Man* set?

6. Which Wayne movie aroused the wrath of anti-war demonstrators?

7. In which film did Wayne give a rendition of *Whiskey, Leave Me Alone*?

8. Wayne appeared in a brief guest spot in which epic Western?

9. Was John Wayne in *The Greatest Story Ever Told*?

10. What was Wayne's last movie?

84. Just Julie

1. What is Julie Andrews' real name?

2. Where was she born?

3. Julie appeared in a West End musical at the age of 12. Title?

4. In which film did Julie play the wife of a missionary?

5. Who was Julie's first husband?

6. Julie won an Oscar for her first movie. Title?

7. Did Christopher Plummer really sing in *The Sound of Music*?

8. Julie starred in Hitchcock's 50th film. Title?

9. In which movie did Beryl Reid appear with Julie?

10. Carol Channing and Beatrice Lillie appeared in supporting roles in a Julie Andrews musical. Title?

85. Citizen Welles

1. What is Orson Welles's full name?

2. Which radio programme by Welles threw America into a panic?

3. Did the Orson Welles classic *Citizen Kane* win him an Oscar?

4. Welles sawed an actress in half in his magic act, then married her. Name?

5. Welles produced and starred in an Eric Ambler spy thriller. Title?

6. Welles was in the John Huston movie *Moby Dick*. True or false?

7. In which detective film did Welles appear with Margaret Lockwood?

8. The Welles movie *The Magnificent Ambersons* was from a novel by whom?

9. Welles's first British film was for director Carol Reed. Title?

10. Which Orson Welles film had a final shoot-out in a Hall of Mirrors?

86. Search your memory (3)

1. In which film did Leslie Caron sing *Hi-Lili Hi-Lo*?

2. What did Jean Harlow and Marilyn Monroe have in common?

3. How old was Rudolph Valentino when he died?

4. *Talk to the Animals* won an Oscar for Best Song in the movie *Dr Dolittle*. Who composed it?

5. In his first film, David Ladd appeared in a Western opposite his father, Alan Ladd. Title?

6. Which Woody Allen film was set in Russia in 1812?

7. For which movie did Ellen Burstyn win an Oscar for Best Actress?

8. Who played Julie Andrews's mother in *The Americanization of Emily*?

9. Name the hit British film in which Dee Hepburn starred.

10. Who played the villain Krisatos in the James Bond movie *For Your Eyes Only*?

87. Saluting Steve

1. What was Steve McQueen's full name?

2. In which Paul Newman film did McQueen appear as an extra named Steven McQueen?

3. Which Western, starring Yul Brynner, gave McQueen his big screen break?

4. In which movie was McQueen nicknamed The Cooler Kid?

5. Ali MacGraw was McQueen's second wife. Who was his first?

6. McQueen did his own driving in *Bullitt*. True or false?

7. In which film about a robbery did Faye Dunaway star with McQueen?

8. Which movie won McQueen an Academy Award nomination?

9. McQueen played the title role in a rodeo story directed by Sam Peckinpah. Title?

10. What was McQueen's last film?

88. La Lucille

1. Lucille Ball is over 70. True or false?

2. When did Lucille's long-running *I Love Lucy* television series start?

3. Lucille played female lead in a Marx Brothers movie. Title?

4. Who did Lucille marry after Desi Arnaz?

5. In which film did Lucille, with 8 children, marry a widower (Henry Fonda) with 10?

6. Lucille starred in the title role of a movie based on a story by Patrick Dennis. Film title?

7. Who played Lucille's husband in *Critic's Choice*?

8. Lucille co-starred with Red Skelton in one of her best-remembered musicals. Title?

9. Gene Kelly directed Lucille in a comedy with Walter Matthau. Title?

10. James Mason appeared with Lucille Ball in the only film produced by Zanra (Arnaz spelt backwards) Productions. Title?

89. Burton-made

1. Name Richard Burton's first film.

2. From whom did Burton take his stage surname?

3. Burton starred for Twentieth Century-Fox in the first CinemaScope film. Title?

4. Who was Burton's first wife?

5. Mike Nichols made his début as director of a Richard Burton — Elizabeth Taylor hit. Title?

6. Who directed Burton in *Look Back in Anger*?

7. In *Staircase*, Burton played one of two ageing homosexuals. Who played the other?

8. Which of Burton's films is listed in *Fifty Worst Movies of All Time*?

9. Did Burton ever win an Oscar?

10. Burton starred in a remake of *Brief Encounter*. Who took the Celia Johnson role?

90. Search your memory (4)

1. In which film were Richard Harris, Roger Moore and Richard Burton soldiers of fortune?

2. Who played the explosives expert in *Force Ten From Navarone*?

3. In which movie did Margaux Hemingway appear with her sister Mariel?

4. Fred Astaire and Judy Garland made only one film together. Title?

5. Who played the title role in *Barry Lyndon*?

6. *Journey's End* was remade with a flying background, starring Malcolm McDowell. Title?

7. Who played Miss Marple in *Murder By Death*?

8. In which movie did Mario Lanza sing *Be My Love*?

9. Who played the escaped convict Magwitch in the remake — with songs — of *Great Expectations*?

10. Name the film in which David Niven played a comic Count Dracula.

91. Mainly Mitchum

1. What is Robert Mitchum's full name?

2. Name Mitchum's first movie.

3. In which movie did Mitchum star with Jack Lemmon and Rita Hayworth?

4. Mitchum starred in a film for which he wrote and recorded the theme song. Movie title?

5. Name the picture Mitchum made in Australia, playing a sheepshearer.

6. In which two movies was Mitchum's co-star Shirley MacLaine?

7. Mitchum co-starred with John Wayne in a notable Western. Title?

8. Mitchum made a movie in Britain with Cary Grant. Title?

9. Robert Mitchum appeared in *The Longest Day*. True or false?

10. Mitchum played private eye Philip Marlowe in which film?

92. Pin-up Betty

1. What was Betty Grable's full name?

2. In which Betty Grable movie were Carmen Miranda and Harry James and his Orchestra featured?

3. Who was Betty Grable's first husband?

4. In which musical were Betty Grable and Alice Faye sisters?

5. Betty Grable starred in a dramatic role in a film with Tyrone Power. Title?

6. In which musical did Betty Grable play a singer from Brooklyn who becomes the toast of London?

7. Betty formed a vaudeville act with Dan Dailey in which picture?

8. In *The Dolly Sisters*, Betty played Jenny Dolly. Who played sister Rosie?

9. What was Betty Grable's last film?

10. How old was Betty when she died in 1973?

93. Director Ford

1. What was John Ford's real name?

2. Name Ford's first talking picture.

3. Which John Ford film set the pattern of the classic Western?

4. Name the John Ford Western in which John Wayne starred as Captain Nathan Brittles.

5. How many Oscars did John Ford win?

6. In which John Ford film did Ward Bond do a parody of Ford himself?

7. Ford directed a British film in which Jack Hawkins starred as a Scotland Yard inspector. Title?

8. Which John Ford picture starred Clark Gable, Ava Gardner and Grace Kelly?

9. Michael Redgrave appeared as the poet William Butler Yeats in a John Ford movie. Title?

10. How old was John Ford when he died in 1973?

94. Search your memory (5)

1. Who took the Fay Wray role in the remake of *King Kong*?

2. In Neil Simon's *Murder By Death*, who played Hercule Poirot?

3. How old was Bing Crosby when he died?

4. Who played the psychiatrist in the movie *Equus*?

5. Name Elvis Presley's first film.

6. Who played the title role in *The Outlaw Josey Wales*?

7. *A Bridge Too Far* was based on a book by whom?

8. Who co-starred in the 1937 version of *A Star Is Born*?

9. Who composed *Ode to Billy Joe* and sang it in the movie of that name?

10. Who played a female KGB agent in the James Bond film *The Spy Who Loved Me*?

95. Know your Bond

1. Name the first James Bond film.

2. In which movie did Roger Moore first play James Bond?

3. Who played 'M' in *Casino Royale*?

4. Donald Pleasence appeared in a Bond film with Sean Connery. Title?

5. Ronnie Corbett appeared in a James Bond film. Title?

6. Who was covered with gold paint in *Goldfinger*?

7. In *Thunderball* a girl called Domino ended up in an inflatable raft with James Bond. Her name?

8. Who sang the title song in *Goldfinger*?

9. Name the actor who played Jaws in *Moonraker*.

10. Who sang the title song in *For Your Eyes Only*?

96. True Brits

1. In *Oliver Twist,* directed by David Lean, who played Bill Sikes?

2. Name the character Peter Sellers played in *I'm All Right, Jack.*

3. Who played Alec Guinness's daughter in *Tunes of Glory*?

4. Which director made his feature-film début with *Saturday Night and Sunday Morning*?

5. What was the offscreen mother-and-daughter connection in *Whistle Down the Wind*?

6. Who said of what: 'It would have been cheaper to lower the Atlantic'?

7. *The Go-Between* was from a novel of the same name. Author?

8. For which film did Tom Courtenay win a British Academy Award as the year's Most Promising Newcomer?

9. In *The Fallen Idol*, who played the little boy?

10. Who played Shell the birdman in the British film success *Odd Man Out*?

97. What a Carry On!

1. What was the first Carry On film?

2. Phil Silvers starred in a Carry On film. Title?

3. Name Frankie Howerd's first Carry On film.

4. Elke Sommer starred in a Carry On film. Title?

5. *Carry On Dick* marked the end of an era for which Carry On stalwart?

6. What was *Carry On At Your Convenience* called overseas?

7. Which Carry On film used the advertising slogan 'A Great Guy With His Chopper'?

8. Which Carry On star went on to work with Laurence Olivier at the National Theatre?

9. Name the first Carry On film made in colour.

10. Harry H. Corbett appeared in only one Carry On film. Title?

98. Search your memory (6)

1. Which well-known actor started in the chorus of *South Pacific*?

2. Who said: 'I just put my feet in the air and move them around'?

3. Which director won Oscars for *From Here to Eternity* and *A Man For All Seasons*?

4. Who was the lady they couldn't kill in *The Ladykillers*?

5. Name Brigitte Bardot's first English-speaking film.

6. Who won a Best Actor Academy Award for the thirties film *The Informer*?

7. Who asked this question of whom: 'What's the bleeding time?'

8. *Evergreen* won an Oscar for Best Song in which Barbra Streisand movie?

9. Name the character Clark Gable portrayed in *Mutiny on the Bounty*.

10. Ernest Borgnine has won one Oscar to date. Name the film.

99. Search your memory (7)

1. Who took a shower in *Psycho*?

2. Who said: 'I started at the top and worked my way down'?

3. In which movie did Groucho Marx play Hugo Z. Hackenbush?

4. Which film did Hitchcock make twice?

5. For which film did Greta Garbo win an Academy Award?

6. Name Charles Chaplin's leading lady in both *Modern Times* and *The Great Dictator*.

7. Who played the heroine in *Raiders of the Lost Ark*?

8. Who is Joe Yule better known as?

9. Who played Sam in *Casablanca*?

10. Name the two movies in which James Coburn portrayed secret agent Flint.

100. You'll never guess! (1)

1. Which hit musical won an Oscar for director Carol Reed?

2. Who was the original choice of director Blake Edwards to play The Pink Panther?

3. Who played Cinderella in *The Slipper and the Rose*?

4. *The Romantic Englishwoman,* starring Glenda Jackson, was from a novel by whom?

5. Who directed the Australian movie *Picnic at Hanging Rock*?

6. George Burns won an Oscar for Best Supporting Actor in a Neil Simon film. Title?

7. Who played vet James Herriot in *All Creatures Great and Small*?

8. Composer Franz Liszt was played by which rock star in *Lisztomania*?

9. Who played the two newspaper reporters in *All the President's Men*?

10. How many Oscars did *One Flew Over the Cuckoo's Nest* win?

101. Calling Connery

1. What is Sean Connery's real first name?

2. Where was he born?

3. What permanent reminder has Connery of his Navy service?

4. Which TV play made Connery a star?

5. Connery was unbilled in a 1957 British film, starring Robert Beatty. Title?

6. Sean Connery was in *The Longest Day*. True or false?

7. In which Hitchcock film did Connery star?

8. Connery starred in a movie with Brigitte Bardot. Title?

9. Fred Zinnemann directed Connery in a picture shot in the Swiss Alps. Title?

10. Name Connery's comeback film as James Bond.

102. Name the movie (1)

1. A gangland boss faces reprisals in a violent
   updating of *Scarface*, set in London's
   East End.

2. A mad American general launches a nuclear
   attack on Russia.

3. A shy girl in a bookstore is chosen by a
   fashion editor and a photographer.

4. An ex-boxer retires to the land of his fathers
   and seeks a wife.

5. Groucho Marx called it 'The only movie I
   ever saw in which the male lead's tits were
   bigger than the female's.'

6. A boy of 10 goes to live with his eccentric
   aunt.

7. A New York cop descends on Marseilles.

8. Ex-convict becomes pop star.

9. A spy chase across Scotland.

10. 'The men . . . the battle . . . the glory . . . the
    world will remember forever!'

103. Name the movie (2)

1. Bob Hope is upstaged by a penguin.

2. A Hungarian girl is groomed to marry the crown prince.

3. Three Walter Matthaus for the price of one.

4. Four children in the Lake District.

5. 'The things you'll see and the things you'll feel are the things that will be part of you as long as you live!'

6. News photographer sees a murder committed.

7. A caretaker goes berserk in a desolate hotel.

8. Villagers take over a branch railway line.

9. Four ship's stowaways on the loose.

10. Timid bank clerk executes bullion robbery.

104. Name the movie (3)

1. Public relations man becomes an alcoholic.

2. Ex-student has affair with wife of father's friend.

3. 'Out of the stirring story of Kipling's India they roar! . . . Three fighting, loving, swaggering sons of the British Battalions!'

4. Borstal boy on the run.

5. Princess falls for a newspaperman.

6. Chicago cop on a mission to London.

7. 'Body of a boy! Mind of a monster! Soul of an unearthly thing!'

8. TV newscaster becomes new Messiah.

9. Ageing boxer refuses to pull last fight.

10. West Indian teacher comes to tough East End school.

105. Classy Cukor

1. Greta Garbo gave probably her best performance in a film directed by George Cukor. Title?

2. Cukor was replaced as director of an MGM epic movie after three weeks. Title?

3. On a visit to England, Cukor discovered a boy who became a star in a classic film he directed. Name the boy.

4. Which musical picture gave Cukor one of his greatest triumphs as a director?

5. Cukor won an Oscar for direction. True or false?

6. Two of Katharine Hepburn's best performances are generally considered to have been in films directed by Cukor. Titles?

7. Cukor directed Garbo in her last screen appearance. Name the film.

8. Which version of Graham Greene's comic novel did Cukor direct as a film?

9. Cukor directed *Romeo and Juliet* for MGM. Who were the stars?

10. Name the last film directed by Cukor.

106. You'll never guess! (2)

1. Who was the voice of Mr Magoo?

2. Who played *Son of Captain Blood*?

3. Shirley Temple sang 'On the Good Ship Lollipop' in which film?

4. Who was Fred Astaire's leading lady in *You Were Never Lovelier*?

5. In which movie did Barbra Streisand sing 'Just Leave Everything To Me'?

6. Who played Pharaoh in *The Ten Commandments*?

7. Who won an Oscar for Best Musical Score in *Jaws*?

8. Who played Cardinal Wolsey in *A Man For All Seasons*?

9. Bob Fosse directed *Cabaret*. True or false?

10. She starred in a film about a ballet dancer, and became a Radio 3 announcer. Name?

107. You'll never guess! (3)

1. Which actor made his film début in *The Maltese Falcon*?

2. Who sang the title song in *The Man With The Golden Gun*?

3. Peter Sellers appeared in *Road to Hong Kong*. True or false?

4. 'Rock Around the Clock' featured in a film starring Sidney Poitier. Title?

5. *Only Two Can Play* was adapted from a Kingsley Amis novel. Title?

6. In which Marx Brothers film did Groucho play Rufus T. Firefly?

7. Who played Woody Allen's wife in *Play It Again, Sam*?

8. The song 'I'm Easy' by Keith Carradine won an Oscar for Best Original Song in which movie?

9. *The Chant of Jimmie Blacksmith* was based on a novel by whom?

10. The music in *Flash Gordon* was by which popular rock band?

108. True or false (1)

1. Joel Grey is the son of comedian Mickey Katz.

2. Stan Laurel was born in Scotland.

3. Patricia Neal won an Oscar for *Hud*.

4. Dudley Moore was in *Alice's Adventures in Wonderland*.

5. Robert Redford won an Oscar for *The Sting*.

6. Gene Hackman was in *Young Frankenstein*.

7. Judy Garland was the middle one of the three Gumm sisters.

8. Stanley Holloway won an Oscar for *My Fair Lady*.

9. Henry Mancini was music arranger for *The Glenn Miller Story*.

10. Mia Farrow is the daughter of Margaret O'Sullivan.

109. True of false (2)

1. Jennifer Jones was in *The Towering Inferno*.

2. Dick Lester directed *Superman: The Movie*.

3. Rosalind Russell played Gypsy Rose Lee in *Gypsy*.

4. Bert Lahr was The Scarecrow in *The Wizard of Oz*.

5. Richard Boone shot Paul Newman in *Hombre*.

6. Shirley Temple is a grandmother.

7. John Williams composed the music for *E.T.*

8. Charles Chaplin won an Oscar for *Limelight*.

9. Faye Dunaway won an Oscar for *Network*.

10. Trini Lopez appeared in *The Dirty Dozen*.

If you MUST look!

Answers to the Picture Quiz are on P.143

1. Catching up on 'Coop'

1. Frank James Cooper. 2. *Sergeant York*.
3. *Vera Cruz*. 4. Audrey Hepburn. 5. *High Noon*.
6. Longfellow Deeds. 7. *Morocco*. 8. Frank
Capra. 9. *The Pride of the Yankees*. 10. *The Naked Edge*.

2. Bushel and a Peck

1. *The Keys of the Kingdom*. 2. *The Yearling*.
3. Celeste Holm. 4. *The Paradine Case*. 5. *To Kill a Mockingbird*. 6. General. 7. *The Gunfighter*.
8. Ahab. 9. *David and Bathsheba*. 10. *Roman Holiday*.

3. Remembering Grace Kelly

1. *The Country Girl*. 2. *To Catch a Thief*.
3. *Dial M for Murder, Rear Window, Suspicion*.
4. *The Swan*. 5. *Mogambo*. 6. *Mogambo*.
7. *Fourteen Hours*. 8. *The Philadelphia Story*.
9. Alfred Hitchcock. 10. 52.

4. Take Ten

1. *Rebecca.* 2. *The VIPs.* 3. Bugs Bunny.
4. Neil Diamond. 5. *In the Heat of the Night.*
6. Lauren Bacall. 7. *Midnight Cowboy.*
8. Abraham Lincoln; 128 films to date. 9. True.
10. Isaac Stern.

5. Beaming in on Bogart

1. DeForest. 2. *Bullets or Ballots.* 3. Ida Lupino.
4. *The Left Hand of God.* 5. Sam Spade. 6. Best
Picture, Best Screenplay, Best Director.
7. *Everybody Goes to Rick's.* 8. Hoagy
Carmichael. 9. *The Barefoot Contessa.* 10. *The
Harder They Fall.*

6. Boning up on Bette

1. *Of Human Bondage.* 2. William Wyler.
3. *Dangerous.* 4. *Jezebel.* 5. *Dark Victory.*
6. Joan Crawford. 7. *Now, Voyager.*
8. *Hollywood Canteen.* 9. *All About Eve.*
10. *The Anniversary.*

7. Latching on to Olivier

1. *The Sleeping Prince.* 2. Archie Rice. 3. *Hamlet.*
4. *Bunny Lake Is Missing.* 5. Douglas MacArthur.
6. Joseph L. Mankiewicz. 7. *Khartoum.* 8. *Fire Over England.* 9. *Queen Christina.* 10. Jill Esmond.

8. Take Ten More

1. *True Grit.* 2. *Sunset Boulevard.* 3. *On Her Majesty's Secret Service.* 4. George Burns.
5. True: he was the ship's captain. 6. *The Outlaw,* starring Jane Russell. 7. *The VIPs.*
8. *Gone With The Wind.* 9. Harry Lime.
10. *Breakfast at Tiffany's.*

9. A Finch of salt

1. *Eureka Stockade.* 2. The Sheriff of Nottingham. 3. *The Story of Gilbert and Sullivan.* 4. *A Town Like Alice.* 5. John Schlesinger. 6. *No Love For Johnnie.* 7. *Network.*
8. *Judith.* 9. *Raid on Entebbe.* 10. *Make Me An Offer.*

10. The answer's a Lemmon

1. *It Should Happen To You.* 2. *Mister Roberts.*
3. Sandy Dennis. 4. Billy Wilder. 5. Best Song.
6. *The Odd Couple.* 7. *Kotch.* 8. *Save the Tiger.*
9. Catherine Deneuve. 10. *The Great Race.*

11. Clueing up on Gary Grant

1. Archie Leach. 2. *Diamond Lil.* 3. Katharine
Hepburn. 4. *The Front Page.* 5. *Suspicion.*
6. Betsy Drake. 7. Blake Edwards. 8. *Charade.*
9. *The Pride and the Passion.* 10. *Night and Day.*

12. Who said it?

1. Frank Sinatra. 2. Alfred Hitchcock. 3. Mae
West. 4. Sophia Loren. 5. Robert Mitchum.
6. Sean Connery. 7. David Niven. 8. Mickey
Rooney. 9. Barbra Streisand. 10. John Wayne.

13. Magic of Montgomery Clift

1. *A Place in the Sun.* 2. Edward Montgomery
Clift. 3. *The Search.* 4. *Red River.* 5. *The
Heiress.* 6. *An American Tragedy.* 7. *From Here
to Eternity.* 8. *Raintree County.* 9. *Judgment at
Nuremberg.* 10. *The Defector.*

14. Educating Rita

1. Margarita Carmen Dolores Cansino. 2. Orson Welles. 3. *Affair in Trinidad*. 4. *Salome*.
5. *Tonight and Every Night*. 6. *The Story on Page One*. 7. *Fire Down Below*. 8. Rogers and Hart. 9. *Miss Sadie Thompson*. 10. *You Were Never Lovelier*.

15. Geeing up on Edward G.

1. Emanuel Goldenberg. 2. Rico. 3. *Dr Ehrlich's Magic Bullet*. 4. Collecting pictures. 5. *A Hole in the Head*. 6. *Key Largo*. 7. *Kid Galahad*. 8. *The Stranger*. 9. *A Boy Is Ten Feet Tall*. 10. *Soylent Green*.

16. Tricky Ten

1. *Play It Again, Sam*. 2. Bernard Schwartz.
3. Errol Flynn. 4. *Ordinary People*. 5. *Fun in Acapulco*. 6. Richard Burton. 7. The Jets and The Sharks. 8. *Funny Girl*. 9. *The King of Marvin Gardens*. 10. *Being There*.

17. Recalling Cagney

1. *The Public Enemy*. 2. Bottom. 3. *The Oklahoma Kid*. 4. Rita Hayworth. 5. True. 6. *The West Point Story*; *Love Me or Leave Me*. 7. *The Bride Came C.O.D.* 8. Ann Sheridan. 9. *The Seven Little Foys*. 10. He didn't.

18. Send for Sophia

1. Carlo Ponti. 2. *Lady L.* 3. *Gold of Naples*. 4. *A Countess From Hong Kong*. 5. *Houseboat*. 6. *The Gun by* C. S. Forester. 7. *Two Women*. 8. *Fall of the Roman Empire*. 9. *Arabesque*. 10. *Attila the Hun; Black Orchid; Heller in Pink Tights*.

19. Fonda memories

1. Five times. 2. Tom Joad. 3. *My Darling Clementine*. 4. *Fort Apache*. 5. *Twelve Angry Men*. 6. True. 7. *The Wrong Man*. 8. *How the West was Won*. 9. *The Longest Day*. 10. *On Golden Pond*.

20. Trickier Ten

1. Misty Rowe. 2. *The Basement Room*.
3. Ginger Rogers. 4. W.C. Fields. 5. *The Graduate*. 6. Reginald Owen. 7. Tatum O'Neal.
8. *Road to Hong Kong*. 9. Alain Delon.
10. Richard Benjamin.

21. Dial B for Barbara

1. *Sorry, Wrong Number*. 2. James M. Cain.
3. *The Plough and the Stars*. 4. *Meet John Doe*.
5. *Titanic*. 6. *Sorry, Wrong Number; Double Indemnity; Ball of Fire; Stella Dallas*.
7. *Roustabout*. 8. *Walk on the Wild Side*.
9. *The Moonlighter*. 10. *The Lady Eve*.

22. Harping on the Marx Brothers

1. Chico, Harpo, Groucho, Gummo, Zeppo.
2. Julius. 3. Minnie Marx. 4. S.J. Perelman.
5. *Duck Soup*. 6. Margaret Dumont. 7. *A Night at the Opera*. 8. *Animal Crackers*. 9. Chico.
10. *Go West*.

23. Checking up on Chaplin

1. Mildred Harris. 2. Walworth. 3. Edna Purviance. 4. *The Tramp*. 5. *The Kid*. 6. Mary Pickford; Douglas Fairbanks, Senior; D.W. Griffith. 7. *City Lights*. 8. Sophia Loren; Marlon Brando. 9. *The Circus*. 10. 88.

24. Even Trickier Ten

1. *20,000 Leagues under the Sea*. 2. Susan Hayward. 3. They all played Sherlock Holmes. 4. *Lust For Life*. 5. *White Heat*. 6. They all featured Ronald Reagan. 7. Cliff Robertson. 8. Humphrey Bogart. 9. Sean Connery. 10. Ringo Starr.

25. The Marvel of Marilyn

1. James Dougherty. 2. *Love Happy*. 3. Tom Ewell. 4. *The Asphalt Jungle*. 5. *No Business Like Show Business*. 6. *Bus Stop*. 7. *Niagara*. 8. Arthur Miller. 9. *Let's Make Love*. 10. *The Misfits*.

26. File on Flynn

1. Leslie Thomson. 2. *Captain Blood.* 3. *Dodge City.* 4. True. 5. *Thank Your Lucky Stars.*
6. Bette Davis. 7. *Too Much, Too Soon.*
8. *The Roots of Heaven.* 9. *The Sun Also Rises.*
10. Jim Corbett.

27. The Scarlett and Rhett Show

1. David O. Selznick. 2. Ashley Wilkes. 3. Vivien Mary Hartley. 4. Olivia de Havilland.
5. Technicolor. 6. Thomas Mitchell. 7. False.
8. Hattie McDaniel. 9. The Yankee captain.
10. False.

28. Heroic Heston

1. *The Greatest Show on Earth.* 2. *El Cid.*
3. *Ben Hur.* 4. *The Agony and the Ecstasy.*
5. *Khartoum.* 6. *The Big Country.* 7. Pierre Boulle. 8. Fraser. 9. *The Three Musketeers; The Four Musketeers.* 10. *The Hawaiians.*

29. On Golden Hepburn

1. *Morning Glory.* 2. *Guess Who's Coming to Dinner?* 3. *The Iron Petticoat.* 4. *Dragon Seed.* 5. False. 6. *Adam's Rib.* 7. *Pat and Mike.* 8. *The Rainmaker.* 9. *Summertime.* 10. It tied with Barbra Streisand for *Funny Girl.*

30. The Lone Granger

1. James Stewart. 2. Elspeth March. 3. *Madonna of the Seven Moons.* 4. *The Man in Grey.* 5. Yehudi Menuhin. 6. Deborah Kerr. 7. *Green Fire.* 8. *Bhowani Junction.* 9. *Scaramouche.* 10. *North to Alaska.*

31. Tell me who

1. Rudolf Nureyev. 2. M. E. Clifton-James. 3. Rod Steiger. 4. Donald O'Connor. 5. Sissy Spacek. 6. Mack Sennett. 7. Mickey Rooney. 8. Alan Bates and Oliver Reed. 9. Joe Pasternak of Esther Williams. 10. Helen Hayes.

32. Mugging up on Mason

1. *The Man in Grey.* 2. Pamela Kellino.
3. *The Seventh Veil.* 4. *Odd Man Out.*
5. *Pandora and the Flying Dutchman.* 6. *The Desert Fox; The Desert Rats.* 7. Danielle Darrieux. 8. *A Star Is Born.* 9. *20,000 Leagues under the Sea.* 10. Humbert Humbert.

33. Just Gene

1. Eugene Curran Kelly. 2. *Thousands Cheer.*
3. *Christmas Holiday.* 4. *Anchors Aweigh.*
5. *The Pirate.* 6. *An American in Paris.*
7. *Marjorie Morningstar.* 8. *Hello, Dolly!*
9. *Inherit the Wind.* 10. *Singin' in the Rain.*

34. A bash at Brando

1. *The Men.* 2. *A Streetcar Named Desire.*
3. *Viva Zapata!* 4. Marc Antony. 5. *The Wild One.* 6. *On the Waterfront.* 7. Desirée. 8. False; he was Sky Masterson. 9. *One-Eyed Jacks.*
10. Trevor Howard.

35. First things first

1. TWA. 2. *Scent of Mystery.* 3. Hitchcock's *Blackmail.* 4. Disney's *Lady and the Tramp.* 5. *Kid Auto Races at Venice.* 6. Katharine Hepburn. 7. *Sonny Boy* from *The Singing Fool.* 8. *Earthquake.* 9. Elmo Lincoln. 10. Clark Gable and Claudette Colbert in *It Happened One Night.*

36. One and only Woody

1. Alan Stewart Konigsberg. 2. *What's New, Pussycat?* 3. Clarinet. 4. *Interiors.* 5. True. 6. *Everything You Always Wanted to Know About Sex (But Were Afraid to Ask).* 7. *Getting Even; Without Feathers; Side Effects.* 8. False; Herbert Ross directed. 9. *A Midsummer Night's Sex Comedy.* 10. *Annie Hall.*

37. Forever Fontaine

1. Olivia de Havilland. 2. *Suspicion.* 3. Brian Aherne. 4. Alfred Hitchcock. 5. Orson Welles. 6. Joseph Cotten. 7. *The Emperor Waltz.* 8. Rossano Brazzi. 9. Japan. 10. *Island in the Sun.*

38. Quite a Ladd

1. Alan Walbridge Ladd. 2. *Boy on a Dolphin*.
3. Daughter-in-law. 4. Veronica Lake. 5. *The
Blue Dahlia*. 6. *My Favourite Brunette*. 7. *Shane*.
8. *Paratrooper*. 9. 50. 10. *The Carpetbaggers*.

39. On the tip of your tongue

1. Jules Munshin. 2. False; it was for Best
Supporting Actress. 3. Maurice Micklewhite.
4. Alec Guinness in *Star Wars*. 5. *The Oscar*.
6. *Doctor No*. 7. Leonard Bernstein. 8. George C.
Scott, for *Patton*. 9. *The Thomas Crown Affair*.
10. Bo Derek.

40. Including Goldwyn out

1. Samuel Goldfisch. 2. Poland. 3. 7.
4. Goldwynisms. 5. Danny Kaye. 6. James
Thurber. 7. Frank Loesser. 8. Jean Simmons.
9. Sidney Poitier. 10. 91.

41. Data on Deborah

1. Scotland. 2. Peter Viertel. 3. False. 4. Portia.
5. *Bonjour Tristesse*. 6. *Separate Tables*.
7. *Casino Royale*. 8. *Quo Vadis?* 9. *The Chalk Garden*. 10. *Heaven Knows, Mr Allison*.

42. Delving into DeMille

1. *The Squaw Man*. 2. Jesse L. Lasky and
Samuel Goldwyn. 3. Cecil Blount DeMille.
4. *Dynamite*. 5. Wild Bill Hickok. 6. Hedy Lamarr
and Victor Mature. 7. Two — in 1923 and 1956.
8. Charlton Heston. 9. Three. 10. *The Ten Commandments*.

43. Ten Toughies

1. *The Private Life of Sherlock Holmes*.
2. *California Suite*. 3. Roger Vadim. 4. David
Prowse. 5. Jack Palance. 6. Harry Nilsson.
7. Faye Dunaway. 8. Laurence Olivier. 9. Jane
Fonda for *Klute*. 10. W. C. Fields.

44. Mindful of Mills

1. *Great Expectations.* 2. Juliet, Hayley, Jonathan. 3. *Swiss Family Robinson.* 4. *Morning Departure.* 5. *Ryan's Daughter.* 6. Mary Hayley Bell. 7. *Tiger Bay.* 8. *Young at Heart.* 9. *Tunes of Glory.* 10. *Oh What a Lovely War.*

45. Best of Bronson

1. Charles Dennis Bunchinsky. 2. *Kid Galahad.* 3. True. 4. *The Dirty Dozen.* 5. Jill Ireland. 6. Joe Valachi. 7. *The Great Escape.* 8. *Death Wish.* 9. *House of Wax.* 10. *Four For Texas.*

46. Reaching for More

1. *A Night to Remember.* 2. Lieutenant Evans. 3. *The Sheriff of Fractured Jaw.* 4. Windmill. 5. *Genevieve.* 6. Paul Brickhill. 7. *The Greengage Summer.* 8. Father Brown. 9. Young Jolyon. 10. Kenny Baker.

47. Who, which, what?

1. Angela Lansbury. 2. *Raging Bull*. 3. Victoria Principal. 4. Ian Charleson. 5. James M. Cain. 6. Cecil Beaton's. 7. Lily Tomlin. 8. Stanley Kubrick. 9. *Airplane!* 10. Sondra Locke.

48. Magnificent Marvin

1. *Cat Ballou*. 2. Major Reisman. 3. *Pocket Money*. 4. Stanley Kramer. 5. *Raintree County*. 6. *Prime Cut*. 7. *The Professionals*. 8. *Paint Your Wagon*. 9. True. 10. *Shout at the Devil*.

49. Brush up your Barbra

1. *The Way We Were* (for the song of that name). 2. *On a Clear Day You Can See Forever*. 3. *Funny Girl*. 4. *What's Up, Doc?* 5. *The Owl and the Pussycat*. 6. *Up the Sandbox*. 7. Paul Newman and Sidney Poitier. 8. Jon Peters. 9. Isaac Bashevis Singer. 10. Yes, a boy, Jason.

50. A note on Bing

1. Harry Lillis Crosby. 2. The Rhythm Boys.
3. *Going My Way*. 4. Dixie Lee. 5. 7. 6. True: he
got the girl from Bob Hope in the last frame.
7. *Holiday Inn*. 8. *Dixie*. 9. *Birth of the Blues*.
10. *A Connecticut Yankee in King Arthur's
Court*.

51. Ten to test you

1. *The Sandpiper*. 2. *Rooster Cogburn*. 3. Peter
Seamus O'Toole. 4. Shirley MacLaine.
5. *Breakheart Pass*. 6. Director Michael Curtiz.
7. Anna Magnani for *The Rose Tattoo*. 8. B.J.
Thomas. 9. Three (in *The Red-haired Alibi*).
10. The same (*The Railway Children*).

52. Looking to your Laurel and Hardy

1. Arthur Stanley Jefferson. 2. *Pardon Us*.
3. 'Here's another nice mess you've gotten us
into!' 4. Fred Karno. 5. Babe. 6. *The Flying
Deuces*. 7. *Fra Diavolo*. 8. *Way Out West*.
9. *Nothing But Trouble*. 10. For creative
pioneering in the field of cinema comedy.

53. Swotting up on Sinatra

1. *Higher and Higher.* 2. Angelo Maggio.
3. *Anchors Aweigh.* 4. Damon Runyon. 5. *High Society.* 6. True; he was a saloon drunk.
7. *Meet Me in Las Vegas.* 8. Lee J. Cobb and Molly Picon. 9. *None But the Brave.*
10. *Ocean's Eleven.*

54. Fangs for the Christopher Lee memory

1. *Moulin Rouge.* 2. *The Dark Avenger.* 3. True; he played Australian Bernard Day. 4. *I, Monster.* 5. *The Curse of Frankenstein.*
6. *Rasputin the Mad Monk.* 7. *The Man With the Golden Gun.* 8. *The Face of Fu Manchu.*
9. *Theatre of Death.* 10. *The Hound of the Baskervilles.*

55. Ten more to test you

1. Maureen O'Sullivan. 2. *Some Came Running.*
3. *A Countess From Hong Kong.* 4. *The Long Hot Summer.* 5. Eric von Stroheim. 6. *The Four Feathers.* 7. Richard Dreyfuss. 8. Edward Fox.
9. David Wark. 10. *All the President's Men* and *Julia.*

56. Close-up on Clint

1. *A Fistful of Dollars.* 2. Rowdy Yates. 3. *Paint Your Wagon.* 4. *Where Eagles Dare.* 5. *Play Misty For Me.* 6. Callahan. 7. *Breezy.* 8. *The Eiger Sanction.* 9. *Every Which Way But Loose.* 10. True.

57. Hope springs eternal

1. Leslie Townes Hope. 2. *Road to Singapore.* 3. *Road to Utopia.* 4. *The Paleface.* 5. *Little Miss Marker.* 6. *The Lemon Drop Kid.* 7. Milly Vitale. 8. *Critic's Choice.* 9. *Boy, Did I Get a Wrong Number!* 10. 5.

58. Memory teasers

1. *Limelight.* 2. Rocky Graziano. 3. *Road to Rio.* 4. Bing Crosby. 5. James Caan. 6. Lynn Redgrave. 7. *Brannigan.* 8. Lee J. Cobb. 9. Gladys Aylward. 10. *The Thief of Baghdad.*

59. Bogarde on the spot

1. Deirek Van Den Bogaerde. 2. *The Servant.*
3. *Darling.* 4. *Victim.* 5. *I Could Go On Singing.*
6. *Song Without End.* 7. *Doctor in the House;
Doctor at Sea; Doctor at Large; Doctor in
Distress.* 8. Von Aschenbach. 9. *The Night
Porter.* 10. *King and Country.*

60. Russell of spring

1. *Billion Dollar Brain.* 2. *Women in Love.*
3. Richard Chamberlain. 4. Sister Jeanne.
5. *The Boy Friend.* 6. *The Savage Messiah.*
7. Robert Powell. 8. Ringo Starr. 9. Elton
John. 10. True.

61. Quiz on Quinn

1. Chihuahua, Mexico. 2. *Parole.* 3. *Viva Zapata!*
and *Lust For Life.* 4. *The Plainsman.*
5. Katharine DeMille. 6. *Zorba the Greek.*
7. *La Strada.* 8. *The Guns of Navarone.*
9. *Requiem For a Heavyweight.* 10. *Lawrence
of Arabia.*

62. More memory teasers

1. *A Matter of Life and Death.* 2. *Hang 'Em High.* 3. Ringling Brothers. 4. *A Touch of Class.* 5. *Beau James.* 6. *Limelight.* 7. Rachmaninov's Second Piano Concerto. 8. Gene Hackman. 9. *High Anxiety.* 10. Al Pacino.

63. Paging Poitier

1. *Cry, the Beloved Country.* 2. *The Blackboard Jungle.* 3. True: *Band of Angels.* 4. *The Defiant Ones.* 5. No; his voice was dubbed by an opera singer. 6. *Lilies of the Field.* 7. *The Slender Thread.* 8. *To Sir, With Love.* 9. *In the Heat of the Night.* 10. *Raisin in the Sun.*

64. Taylor-made

1. *National Velvet.* 2. Nicky Hilton. 3. *X, Y and Zee.* 4. *Reflections in a Golden Eye.* 5. *Butterfield 8* and *Who's Afraid of Virginia Woolf?* 6. *Giant.* 7. False. 8. *The Comedians.* 9. True; she was one of the Christian martyrs fleeing from the lions in the Colosseum. 10. *A Place in the Sun* and *Giant.*

65. Raising Caine

1. *Zulu*. 2. *Alfie*. 3. *Alfie* and *Sleuth*. 4. *Dressed to Kill*. 5. *The Ipcress File; Funeral in Berlin; Billion Dollar Brain*. 6. *Pulp*. 7. *The Wilby Conspiracy*. 8. Sean Connery. 9. Pele. 10. *The Last Valley*.

66. Still more memory teasers

1. *Here Comes the Groom*. 2. Liquorice. 3. Estelle Parsons. 4. Gregory Peck. 5. *Monsieur Beaucaire*. 6. *The Joker Is Wild*. 7. Kirk Douglas. 8. Roy Scheider. 9. Popeye Doyle. 10. *The Music Box*.

67. Label it Huston

1. Marcellus. 2. *The Maltese Falcon*. 3. *The Treasure of Sierra Madre*. 4. *The Asphalt Jungle*. 5. Humphrey Bogart. 6. Jose Ferrer. 7. *Key Largo*. 8. True. 9. *Fat City*. 10. Arthur Miller.

68. Just Jane

1. Seymour. 2. Donald Sutherland. 3. *They Shoot Horses, Don't They?* 4. Tom Hayden. 5. *The Chapman Report.* 6. George Segal. 7. *The China Syndrome.* 8. *California Suite.* 9. *Coming Home.* 10. *Julia.*

69. Mad Mel

1. Melvin Kaminsky. 2. Sid Caesar. 3. *The Producers.* 4. *The Muppet Movie.* 5. *The Critic* and *The Producers.* 6. *The Twelve Chairs.* 7. *Blazing Saddles.* 8. *Young Frankenstein.* 9. *Silent Movie.* 10. *History of the World, Part I.*

70. Try these for size

1. *The Lost Weekend.* 2. A car crash. 3. Vangelis. 4. Henry De Vere Stacpoole. 5. *Brubaker.* 6. Nancy Walker. 7. Warner Oland. 8. Scotland. 9. *Mary Poppins.* 10. Jerome Kern.

71. Beaming in on Burt

1. Burton Leon Reynolds. 2. *Deliverance*.
3. *Sharky's Machine*. 4. *The Cannonball Run*.
5. Two; *Smokey and the Bandit* and *Smokey and the Bandit II*. 6. *Silent Movie*. 7. No. 8. *The Man Who Loved Cat Dancing*. 9. True. 10. *Hooper*.

72. Be sure of Shelley

1. Shirley Schrift. 2. *Meet Danny Wilson*.
3. *Winchester 73*. 4. Vittorio Gassman.
5. Montgomery Clift. 6. *Night of the Hunter*.
7. *The Diary of Anne Frank* and *A Patch of Blue*. 8. *Bloody Mama*. 9. *Who Slew Auntie Roo?* 10. Jack Albertson.

73. Know your Niven

1. *Bachelor Mother*. 2. *The Moon Is Blue*.
3. *Separate Tables*. 4. *The Road to Hong Kong*.
5. *The Moon's a Balloon*. 6. *Spitfire*. 7. *Bonnie Prince Charlie*. 8. *The Toast of New Orleans*.
9. *My Man Godfrey*. 10. Phileas Fogg.

74. Who said this?

1. Michael Caine. 2. Anthony Quinn. 3. James
Dean. 4. Director Josh Logan. 5. Charlton
Heston. 6. Stewart Granger. 7. Boris Karloff.
8. George Burns. 9. Barbra Streisand. 10. Paul
Newman.

Picture Quiz

1. Alec Guinness. 2. Myrna Loy, left, and Gloria
Swanson. 3. Lisa Harrow. 4. Jack Warden.
5. Cyril Cusack. 6. Anthony Quayle and Donald
Pleasence.

75. Astaire is born

1. His sister Adele. 2. *The Gay Divorce*. 3. *The
Band Wagon*. 4. *Wedding Bells* (*Royal Wedding*
in U.S.) 5. *Daddy Long Legs*. 6. *Finian's Rainbow*.
7. His contribution to musicals. 8. *The Barkleys
of Broadway*. 9. *On the Beach*. 10. *The Towering
Inferno*.

76. Recalling Bacall

1. *Harper's Bazaar.* 2. *To Have and Have Not.*
3. *Key Largo.* 4. Jason Robards. 5. *The Big Sleep.*
6. Marilyn Monroe and Betty Grable. 7. *Written on the Wind.* 8. *Designing Woman.* 9. *Harper.*
10. *Murder on the Orient Express.*

77. Preminger presents

1. *Laura.* 2. *Stalag 17.* 3. *The Moon Is Blue.*
4. *River of No Return.* 5. *Carmen Jones* and *Porgy and Bess.* 6. Kim Novak. 7. False; Dalton Trumbo wrote the screenplay. 8. Allen Drury.
9. *The Cardinal.* 10. *Bunny Lake Is Missing.*

78. Search your memory (1)

1. John Hurt. 2. *The Fiendish Plot of Dr Fu Manchu.* 3. *For Your Eyes Only.* 4. Robin Williams. 5. Jake La Motta. 6. *Tess.* 7. *Tribute.*
8. *Wholly Moses!* 9. Peter Lorre. 10. *Xanadu.*

79. My Guinness!

1. *The Mudlark.* 2. Anthony Newley. 3. *Kind Hearts and Coronets.* 4. They both starred in films called *The Detective.* 5. *The Bridge on the River Kwai.* 6. *Last Holiday.* 7. *The Bridge on the River Kwai* and *Tunes of Glory.* 8. *The Lavender Hill Mob.* 9. *The Swan.* 10. Ben Kenobi.

80. Garland for Judy

1. Frances Gumm. 2. *Pigskin Parade.* 3. Sophie Tucker. 4. *Thoroughbreds Don't Cry.* 5. David Rose. 6. *The Wizard of Oz.* 7. *Meet Me in St Louis.* 8. Betty Hutton. 9. *Thousands Cheer.* 10. *The Pirate.*

81. Know your Newman

1. *The Silver Chalice.* 2. Pier Angeli. 3. *Cool Hand Luke.* 4. *The Hustler.* 5. False; only Joanne has. 6. *Cat on a Hot Tin Roof.* 7. Motor-racing. 8. *Hud.* 9. *Rachel, Rachel.* 10. *The Sting.*

82. Search your memory (2)

1. *Sextette*. 2. Bernard Lee. 3. *Melvin and Howard*. 4. *Silver Dream Racer*. 5. Shelley Duvall. 6. True. 7. Peter O'Toole. 8. John Travolta. 9. *Papa's Delicate Condition*. 10. Kid Galahad.

83. The Duke

1. Marion Michael Morrison. 2. *Stagecoach*. 3. *The Alamo*. 4. *True Grit*. 5. Ireland. 6. *The Green Berets*. 7. *Hatari!* 8. *How the West Was Won*. 9. Yes; in a long shot as a Roman centurion. 10. *The Shootist*.

84. Just Julie

1. Julia Elizabeth Wells. 2. Walton-on-Thames. 3. *Starlight Roof*. 4. *Hawaii*. 5. Tony Walton. 6. *Mary Poppins*. 7. No; his voice was dubbed. 8. *Torn Curtain*. 9. *Star!* 10. *Thoroughly Modern Millie*.

85. Citizen Welles

1. George Orson Welles. 2. An adaptation of *The War of the Worlds*. 3. Yes; for Best Original Screenplay. 4. Rita Hayworth. 5. *Journey Into Fear*. 6. True; he played a preacher. 7. *Trent's Last Case*. 8. Booth Tarkington. 9. *The Third Man*. 10. *The Lady From Shanghai*.

86. Search your memory (3)

1. *Lili*. 2. Each made her last film with Clark Gable. 3. 31. 4. Leslie Bricusse. 5. *The Proud Rebel*. 6. *Love and Death*. 7. *Alice Doesn't Live Here Anymore*. 8. Joyce Grenfell. 9. *Gregory's Girl*. 10. Julian Glover.

87. Saluting Steve

1. Terence Steven McQueen. 2. *Somebody Up There Likes Me*. 3. *The Magnificent Seven*. 4. *The Great Escape*. 5. Neile Adams. 6. True. 7. *The Thomas Crown Affair*. 8. *The Sand Pebbles*. 9. *Junior Bonner*. 10. *The Hunter*.

88. La Lucille

1. True; she was born in 1911. 2. 1951. 3. *Room Service*. 4. Gary Morton. 5. *Yours, Mine and Ours*. 6. *Mame*. 7. Bob Hope. 8. *DuBarry Was a Lady*. 9. *A Guide For the Married Man*. 10. *Forever, Darling*.

89. Burton-made

1. *The Last Days of Dolwyn*. 2. Philip Burton, his schoolmaster. 3. *The Robe*. 4. Sybil Williams. 5. *Who's Afraid of Virginia Woolf?* 6. Tony Richardson. 7. Rex Harrison. 8. *The Assassination of Trotsky*. 9. No; he has been nominated seven times. 10. Sophia Loren.

90. Search your memory (4)

1. *The Wild Geese*. 2. Edward Fox. 3. *Lipstick*. 4. *Easter Parade*. 5. Ryan O'Neal. 6. *Aces High*. 7. Elsa Lanchester. 8. *Toast of New Orleans*. 9. James Mason. 10. *Vampira*.

91. Mainly Mitchum

1. Robert Charles Mitchum. 2. *Hoppy Serves a Writ*. 3. *Fire Down Below*. 4. *Thunder Road*; the song was *The Ballad of Thunder Road*. 5. *The Sundowners*. 6. *Two For the Seesaw* and *What a Way to Go!* 7. *El Dorado*. 8. *The Grass Is Greener*. 9. True. 10. *Farewell, My Lovely*.

92. Pin-up Betty

1. Ruth Elizabeth Grable. 2. *Springtime in the Rockies*. 3. Jackie Coogan. 4. *Tin Pan Alley*. 5. *A Yank in the RAF*. 6. *Sweet Rosie O'Grady*. 7. *Mother Wore Tights*. 8. June Haver. 9. *How to Be Very Very Popular*. 10. 56.

93. Director Ford

1. Sean Augustine O'Feeney. 2. *Napoleon's Barber* (1928). 3. *Stagecoach*. 4. *She Wore A Yellow Ribbon*. 5. Six. 6. *The Wings of Eagles*. 7. *Gideon's Day*. 8. *Mogambo*. 9. *Young Cassidy*. 10. 78.

94. Search your memory (5)

1. Jessica Lange. 2. James Coco. 3. 73. 4. Richard Burton. 5. *Love Me Tender*. 6. Clint Eastwood. 7. Cornelius Ryan. 8. Fredric March and Janet Gaynor. 9. Bobbie Gentry. 10. Barbara Bach.

95. Know your Bond

1. *Dr No*. 2. *Live and Let Die*. 3. John Huston. 4. *You Only Live Twice*. 5. *Casino Royale*. 6. Shirley Eaton. 7. Claudine Auger. 8 Shirley Bassey. 9. Richard Kiel. 10. Sheena Easton.

96. True Brits

1. Robert Newton. 2. Fred Kite. 3. Susannah York. 4. Karel Reisz. 5. Hayley Mills starred; her mother, Mary Hayley Bell, wrote the screen adaptation. 6. Lord Grade of *Raise the Titanic*. 7. L. P. Hartley. 8. *The Loneliness of the Long Distance Runner*. 9. Bobby Henrey. 10. F. J. McCormick.

97. What a Carry On!

1. *Carry On Sergeant.* 2. *Carry On . . . Follow That Camel.* 3. *Carry On Doctor.* 4. *Carry On Behind.* 5. Sid James. 6. *Carry On Round the Bend.* 7. *Carry On Henry.* 8. Jim Dale. 9. *Carry On Cruising.* 10. *Carry On Screaming.*

98. Search your memory (6)

1. Sean Connery. 2. Fred Astaire. 3. Fred Zinnemann. 4. Katie Johnson. 5. *Doctor at Sea.* 6. Victor McLaglen. 7. James Robertson Justice of Dirk Bogarde in *Doctor in the House.* 8. *A Star Is Born.* 9. Fletcher Christian. 10. *Marty.*

99. Search your memory (7)

1. Janet Leigh. 2. Orson Welles. 3. *A Day at the Races.* 4. *The Man Who Knew Too Much;* in 1934 and 1955. 5. No special film; but she was awarded a special Oscar in 1954. 6. Paulette Goddard. 7. Karen Allen. 8. Mickey Rooney. 9. Dooley Wilson. 10. *Our Man Flint* and *In Like Flint.*

100. You'll never guess! (1)

1. *Oliver!* 2. Peter Ustinov. 3. Gemma Craven.
4. Thomas Wiseman. 5. Peter Weir. 6. *The Sunshine Boys*. 7. Simon Ward. 8. Roger Daltrey.
9. Robert Redford and Dustin Hoffman. 10. Five.

101. Calling Connery

1. Tommy. 2. Edinburgh. 3. Two tattoos on his right forearm. 4. *Requiem For A Heavyweight*.
5. *Time Lock*. 6. True. 7. *Marnie*. 8. *Shalako*.
9. *Five Days One Summer*. 10. *Never Say Never Again*.

102. Name the movie (1)

1. *The Long Good Friday*. 2. *Dr Strangelove*.
3. *Funny Face*. 4. *The Quiet Man*. 5. *Samson and Delilah*. 6. *Mame*. 7. *French Connection II*.
8. *Jailhouse Rock*. 9. *The Thirty-nine Steps*.
10. *Waterloo*.

103. Name the movie (2)

1. *My Favourite Blonde*. 2. *The Swan*. 3. *Plaza Suite*. 4. *Swallows and Amazons*. 5. *Judgment At Nuremberg*. 6. *Rear Window*. 7. *The Shining*. 8. *The Titfield Thunderbolt*. 9. *Monkey Business*. 10. *The Lavender Hill Mob*.

104. Name the movie (3)

1. *Days of Wine and Roses*. 2. *The Graduate*. 3. *Gunga Din*. 4. *The Loneliness of the Long Distance Runner*. 5. *Roman Holiday*. 6. *Brannigan*. 7. *I Was a Teenage Frankenstein*. 8. *Network*. 9. *The Set Up*. 10. *To Sir, With Love*.

105. Classy Cukor

1. *Camille*. 2. *Gone With The Wind*. 3. Freddie Bartholomew. The film was *David Copperfield*. 4. *My Fair Lady*. 5. False. 6. *Holiday* and *The Philadelphia Story*. 7. *Two-Faced Woman*. 8. *Travels With My Aunt*. 9. Norma Shearer and Leslie Howard. 10. *Rich And Famous,* starring Candice Bergen and Jacqueline Bisset.

106. You'll never guess!(2)

1. Jim Backus. 2. Sean Flynn; son of Errol.
3. *Bright Eyes*. 4. Rita Hayworth. 5. *Hello, Dolly!*
6. Cedric Hardwicke. 7. John Williams. 8. Orson
Welles. 9. True. 10. Moira Shearer.

107. You'll never guess! (3)

1. Sydney Greenstreet. 2. Lulu. 3. True. 4. *The Blackboard Jungle*. 5. 'That Uncertain Feeling.'
6. *Duck Soup*. 7. Susan Anspach. 8. *Nashville*.
9. Thomas Keneally. 10. Queen.

108. True or false (1)

1. True. 2. False; in Ulverston, England. 3. True.
4. True; as the Dormouse. 5. False. 6. True.
7. False; the youngest. 8. False. 9. True. 10. False;
Maureen O'Sullivan.

109. True or false (2)

1. True. 2. False; he directed *Superman 2*.
3. False; Natalie Wood was Gypsy Rose Lee.
Rosalind played her mother. 4. False; Ray Bolger
was. Lahr was the Cowardly Lion. 5. True.
6. True. 7. True. 8. True; for his musical score.
9. True. 10. True.